Only servants

Only servants

A view of the place, responsibilities and ministries of elders in local churches

Clifford C. Pond

Foreword by John Benton

GRACE PUBLICATIONS TRUST
139 Grosvenor Avenue
London N5 2NH
England

General Editors:
H. J. Appleby
J. P. Arthur M.A.

ISBN 0 946462 24 0

Distributed by
EVANGELICAL PRESS
12 Wooler Street
Darlington
Co. Durham DL1 1RQ
England

Bible quotations are from the New International Version (© Hodder &
Stoughton)

Cover design and photograph - Lawrence L. Evans

Printed in Great Britain at the Bath Press, Avon.

To Muriel, Beryl and Eunice

Contents

Foreword

This book is about eldership and in particular the need for plural eldership, a team of elders, in leading a local church. I want to commend Clifford's work both to churches which do not as yet have plural eldership and to those which already have such.

'I don't feel very cared for.' Those are very poignant words when they come from a church member. Of course, some people, who live on self- pity, will never feel cared for no matter how much attention is lavished on them. But sometimes such words are genuine and show up real deficiencies in the oversight of a church. I wonder how many people in our churches feel like that? They don't expect to be wrapped around in cotton wool, or want to be smothered under heavy-handed authoritarianism, but they do want to feel cared for by the church leadership. I am not saying that where there is no plural eldership there is no care. Many pastors do a wonderful job single-handed. But that care can be improved and the pressures of single-handed ministry greatly reduced where eldership becomes team-work. That is why I would commend this book to churches where plural eldership has yet to be introduced. I think Clifford's work is unique in not only bringing out the Biblical principles concerning this very important subject but in tackling many common practical aspects entailed in the setting up and proper functioning of a team of elders.

All right, I have said why churches without elderships need to read this book but why commend it to churches where a plural eldership is already in place? A plural eldership needs to be kept on its toes. Having a team of elders is not a panacea for a church. It can bring other problems with it compared with the one pastor model of leadership. For members of a church bad leadership is like the frustration of driving behind a slow, wide lorry on a narrow winding country lane when you have to get somewhere urgently. You cannot see where you are going, you cannot see to overtake and you cannot use your car to its full potential. Sadly, sometimes the setting up of plural eldership has just made the lorry wider and even slower. It should be an urgent matter with us that we should be the best we can be for Christ as churches. There needs to be direction and decision in the leadership of the church. Leadership in a church is not just about care and control but about guiding, encouraging and developing the full potential of the church.

Compared with the single pastor system a team of elders can lead to decision making becoming far more ponderous and slow with a number of men consulting together rather than one man coming to a conclusion. Again, a unified eldership is an enormous blessing to a church, but a divided eldership saps the strength of the church and can wreak havoc, leaving the church members desperately discouraged, sitting behind a wide load lorry which fills the road and has broken down. A team of elders does not guarantee automatic benefits. Elderships need to be kept on their toes. That is why I would commend this book to churches which have existing plural elderships.

You will find many years of study and experience wisely distilled into the pages of this book. Clifford holds up a mirror for eldership teams and gets us to take a good look at ourselves, and then provides words of insight and encouragement to go forward.

It gives me special pleasure to write this foreword as I personally am very indebted to the writer. Clifford was the previous 'pastor' of the church in Guildford where I now minister, and had done all the hard graft of bringing the church to set up plural eldership in the years before I came. As a young, inexperienced preacher joining the eldership I needed to be nurtured in my work just as much as anyone else in the church. I needed the experience of older, wiser men alongside me in the eldership to gently stop me going off on youthful tangents. The church needed the confidence of knowing that when the new man made mistakes there were other elders to put him straight, encourage him and lead him on. Looking back now over nearly eleven years we can see that much of the blessing we have experienced as a church has been the fruit of that foundation which Clifford laid in plural eldership.

John Benton
Guildford
29 January 1991

Introduction

'Why do we have to suffer all these changes?'
'We were all right as we were.'
'Who makes the decisions now?'
'Church members are only rubber stamps.'
'How do elders and deacons relate to each other?'
'You can't run a church with a committee.'

These are things church members are saying; more seriously, they reflect tensions, divisions and resignations among the churches.

How has this come about?

In the seventies a desire grew throughout the evangelical world to find new structures which would help the church to fulfil its calling before God.

Also, in the face of the laxity and permissiveness in so much of the church, many Christians have had a longing for doctrinal and moral purity and biblical discipline, a longing for a restrained life-style in the church, and for a caring community for people in need.

With this motivation, many churches have tried to develop forms of government which they hope will promote life. Some have done this because of the lack of community and genuine shepherding in so much of the church.

(In *Freedom and Discipleship* Jerram Barrs. I.V.P)

This is true; but upheavals have also taken place in society generally running parallel to the changes among the churches, and there is always some inter-action between the world and the churches. But among the churches the reasons for change have been primarily spiritual and biblical. There has also been inter-action between charismatic influences and traditional church life and a great deal of conforming to new fashions. Nevertheless in and through all these things we have been driven back to Scripture to retain what harmonises with the Word, to take on board new insights, and to reject that which is superficial, compromising and ineffective in modern evangelicalism.

From the 16th century Presbyterians have provided for a number of elders to oversee the life of each local congregation. More recently the Brethren have also followed this pattern. Soon after the Second World War, many independent evangelical churches became convinced that plurality of elders is indeed in harmony with the New Testament but, in some cases, what they thought would be a great blessing has in practice brought discord and division. In trying to write something helpful about all this from the standpoint of elders, I pray the Lord to forbid that this book adds to the problems of any local church. Rather may it be an instrument of light, peace and joy and for the preparation of 'God's people for works of service' (Ephesians 4:12). I have great love and respect for those who will differ from me in some of the things I will say. I plead we may discuss them with grace and humility. None of us has a perfect understanding of the Scriptures, and if we are honest we have to admit that neither traditional structures nor recent changes are without problems. Furthermore we have all made ghastly mistakes and continue to do so.

We must not spend too much time dealing with church structures and organisation.

> We are so absorbed with our arguments about church order, authority, forms of worship and denominationalism, that we are missing the tremendous implications of the gospel.
>
> (T. A. Steen, *Revival Digest* — Summer 1989)

We must heed that warning. If all we are concerned about is to achieve good church organisation, like a well-oiled machine going nowhere, we should stop now. There is value in soldiers under training running on the spot, but not as an end in itself; it must be with a view to action. A healthy church is one that receives and obeys instruction from the Lord, the Head of the church, both as to its structure and its objectives. The objectives are to prepare the people of God for the work of God and ultimately for eternal glory. The great reason for a local church to exist is to spread the gospel locally, in the nation, and in the world. Organisation and administration must not hinder this process but rather be a means to its fulfilment. Organisation must make action more effective; if it does not do so it has lost its way. Administration should be an aid to the spread of the gospel; if it is not it should be dismantled and reconstructed.

I rejoice that the Lord is pleased to bless churches with widely differing forms of administration. But we must not conclude from this that these things are unimportant. They can help or hinder the progress of the gospel, the nurturing of new converts, the maturing of believers, and a true understanding of sound doctrine.

> The certainty that some day the church would be glorified did not any way deter the apostles from striving to improve and set in order the condition of the church as they found it, for the leaders of the New Covenant community recognised that the prosperity of the gospel in the world is closely related to the condition of the visible church that proclaims it. To them, loving Christ and keeping his commandments meant not only attending to the welfare of individual Christians, but also to the corporate welfare of those who comprise the body of Christ. This meant, first and foremost, diligence in finding and training leaders who would be biblically qualified to oversee the collective life of Christ's flock.
> (Roger O. Beardmore, *Shepherding God's flock,* Sprinkle Publications)

The situation in Crete at the time of Titus was grim; social and moral conditions were similar to those in the twentieth century western world. But in Paul's letter to Titus his first concern was to get the leadership and relationships within the church sorted out (Titus 1:5-9). We can be sure this was with a view to effective gospel outreach and we can also be sure the subject of organisation did not occupy endless church time; in the long run good organisation saves time.

Again the situation in Jerusalem (Acts 6:1-7) required a simple structure to be established. The right people were put into the right places, and the poor Grecian widows were given a fair deal. Then we read: 'So the word of God spread. The number of disciples in Jerusalem increased rapidly' (Acts 6:7). I pray that the same kind of spiritual blessings will flow from our attempts to establish healthy churches and that this book will be one means to that end.

Some things here may seem to be matters of common sense, so obvious as not to need the space given to them. I would plead that though this may appear to be so, all too often problems have arisen and divisions created for want of observing them. Those who are strong in such matters please bear with those who are weak (Romans 15:1).

Churches vary considerably in size, background, history, tradition and available talents, and for this reason it is difficult to cater for all 'shapes and sizes'. I have tried to bear in mind small churches in which the 'pastor does everything'. I honour such churches and the dedication of the men and their people. I pray the Lord to give them such increase that they will know the privilege of facing the problems of growth!

Happily many churches are growing and I hope what I say here may help them to avoid mistakes others of us have made.

Some readers may find a certain amount of idealism here; I make no apology for that. A popular magazine once had as its motto 'Look up and aim high.' Let us reach for the sky even if we only manage to scale Everest! Nevertheless we all have much to learn and no structure should be so idealised as to be beyond modification.

Please bear with a certain amount of repetition. I have not corrected this but rather tried to make each chapter complete in itself for easier reference. I hope the questions at the end of each chapter will stimulate discussion among elders and in the churches, even if the conclusions you reach are not the same as mine.

A large number of articles have been written in recent years about eldership and the administration of local churches, and small study groups have published papers, and individual local churches have issued study notes. I have taken the liberty of using this material freely. Among writers I have widely used are: John Benton, Robin Dowling, Jack Hoad, and Peter Masters. If others recognise their original thoughts and I have not credited them please forgive me in the spirit that 'we are God's fellow workers' (1 Corinthians 3:9).

Questions

1 Would it be possible to examine the life of your church in the light of Scripture without either aversion to change or determination to change for the sake of it?

2 When last did such an examination take place in your church; is now the right time?

1.
Where have we come from?

Independent evangelical churches of the twentieth century are the product of gradual development since our Lord returned to glory. There has been much sifting of truth from error, constant attempts at reformation and the influence of strong personalities for good or ill.

As we will see in chapter two New Testament churches submitted to Jesus Christ as their Lord and Head. Each church was independently responsible to the Lord and was guided by him in everything including the appointment of its own leaders. This very soon gave way to schemes arising from human wisdom and ambitions. Some elders, who became known as bishops, sought to have pre-eminence over others. We can see the beginnings of this in the New Testament, for example, 'Diotrephes, who loves to be first' (3 John 9). Leaders who had charge of influential congregations began to exalt themselves above others. This led in later centuries to the idea of a pope in Rome with supreme authority. All this resulted in the erosion of the practice of the early church and there arose a system of government from outside the local churches. This state of affairs continues in Roman Catholic and Anglican churches today, and in other groups where direction is received from some ecclesiastical body outside the local church, or where decisions are made on behalf of local churches.

But it is doubtful if there was ever a time throughout the Christian era when there were no independent evangelical churches. This has been helpfully sketched by Jack Hoad, (*The Baptist* pages 25-26, Grace Publications):

...The departure of the early churches from their initial New Testament character was not a sudden apostasy but a 'slow drift away from its living spontaneity and simplicity to preserving the genius of the Christian movement by enclosing it in an elaborate hierarchical system. In attempting this they transformed it into an inflexible, architectured order of vast uniformity, very startlingly unlike the New Testament original ' as G.O.Griffith says ... Again quoting Griffith, 'the early stream of evangelical faith passed out of sight and became an underflow, now and then, gushing upward in various movements of protest — upbursts in which earthy elements mingled with the pure springs '.

(Dr. Hoad is quoting from *A pocket history of the Baptist Movement*, Kingsgate, London).

There is no doubt that many of the independent churches and groups of churches that protested against the tendency to centralised organisation did have 'earthy elements'. Most, if not all of them, embraced one or another kind of heresy, or eccentricity. But their aim was to restore a biblical order of churches composed of born again and, usually, baptized believers, independently responsible to Christ alone. These groups of churches we know by such names as Montanists (2nd century), Novatians (3rd century), Donatists (4th century) and Paulicians (7th century). In Britain there were active bible-based churches that opposed the domination of Rome until 'the action of Augustine of Canterbury begun in 596 A.D. almost extinguished the old British churches and stamped a tight Roman or Western Catholic grip on Christianity in this land' (*The Baptist*, page 34).

Up to the time of the Reformation (16th century) leaders arose advocating biblical Christianity such as Peter of Bruys and Peter Waldo (12th century), John Wycliffe (14th century), and Jan Huss (15th century). People we know as Anabaptists arose in the 15th century and sad to say, they were opposed and persecuted by the Reformers, Luther, Calvin, Cranmer and others. Anabaptists believed that the church in the New Testament was local, independent and comprised regenerate, baptized believers only.

From the time of the Reformation there came Presbyterians and others like them who rejected the rule of bishops. They were governed by councils outside their local churches, but the councils were comprised of presbyters freely chosen by the people. To many believers this system still fell short of the independency of local churches as seen in the New Testament. John Milton said: 'New presbyter is but old priest writ large.' It is often asked why the reformers did not settle the issue of church order as they did the matter of justification by faith only. It is surely unreasonable to expect more of those great men than the massive foundation in salvation doctrine they achieved.

In this country there arose groups such as Congregationalists, Independents, Baptists, and later Brethren, who with some variations in practice were self-governing, with their own appointed leaders under the Lordship of Christ. This is the situation among independent, evangelical churches today, going under a variety of labels.

Within such churches there have been a variety of provisions for leadership. Some have followed Calvin with a fourfold leadership of pastors, teachers (also called doctors) elders and deacons. Others have been led by men called apostles; some have had both apostles and prophets; a number of such groups are to be seen again today.

In recent times the majority of independent evangelical churches have had one pastor assisted by a group of deacons, but an increasing number of these churches have become convinced that they should be led by a group of elders along with a group of deacons. This has given rise to confusion and a crisis of authority in many places. Before we tackle those matters directly we must first make sure of our ground as independent churches.

Questions

1   What can churches from other historical backgrounds teach us about the leadership of churches?
2   Is the current tendency to change the result of:
     an historical process?
     a desire to be in the fashion?
     more light on Scripture?
     learning from mistakes in the past?
     anti-authoritarianism?

2.
Independent churches

The people of God in Old Testament times were identified with the nation of Israel. The church was the nation — the nation was the church. This is the pattern from which the idea of a national church comes and along with it the control of local churches by national or regional authorities. Sometimes the authority is political. For example, the British Parliament exercises some control over the Church of England, having a say in such matters as appointing bishops or the revision of the Prayer Book. In other cases control from outside the local church is exercised by church leaders in councils or synods as with our Presbyterian friends. These systems are built upon Old Testament structures and they do not take account of the clear differences between New Testament churches and the regime of Old Testament times. This is the principle behind the refusal of many independent churches in communist countries and others to register with the State. They will not suffer political interference in their local church affairs.

But even in Old Testament days the tribes frequently acted independently of each other; more especially a 'remnant' within Israel who began to be recognised as people who were true to the Lord (Jeremiah 23:3; Malachi 3:14-17) while the rest of the nation was unfaithful to him. It was to this remnant that the Lord looked and he heard their prayers. These were the true Israel (Romans 9:6) and all believers in Jesus Christ are one with them (Galatians 3:13-14; 29), so that the continuity from the Old to the New Testament is not structural but spiritual. This is confirmed by the fact that the covenant blessings promised in Jeremiah (31:33-34) are applied by the writer to the Hebrews (8:7-13) to New Testament believers.

In the nation of Israel God has given us many pictures of spiritual truth. The nation, the tabernacle and temple, the priesthood, and the sacrifices all provide us with valuable pictures of the work of Jesus Christ and the life of his people (1 Peter 2:4-10). All these aspects of Old Testament life and worship pointed on to Jesus Christ and the spiritual body of believers, his church. It is therefore a mistake to carry them over physically and materially, to New Testament times.

In the New Testament, the churches made up of born again believers in Jesus Christ existed independently with no external control. Jesus Christ was their Lord and he was present to preside over their gatherings (Matthew 18:20). The 1966 Affirmation of Faith gathers up the evidence like this:

It is the duty of all believers, walking in the fear of the Lord, to unite with local churches, for their own sanctification, and the maintenance of gospel witness. Such churches, having the presence of Christ as head, are responsible to him for their own administration, and in this respect are independent of every other form of control, whether of Church or State. They have the fulness of God, and to them is committed the stewardship of the Gospel, the defence of the truth, the discipline of disorderly members, the appointment of officers, and the administration of the ordinances. Matthew 18:15-20; Ephesians 1:22-23; Acts 13:1-4; 1 Corinthians 5; 2 Thessalonians 3:6; 1 John 4:1; Revelation 2 and 3.

(*We Believe,* page 30, Grace Publications Trust)

Each church was responsible for its own administration, discipline, ministry, fellowship and evangelism. Letters in the New Testament, which were the authoritative word of God, were addressed to local churches and they were expected to carry out the instructions in those letters whether to love each other, to discipline unruly members,to defend and proclaim the gospel, or to appoint their leaders. There was only one external authority, namely, the apostles. But even those apostles directed the local churches to deal with their own problems (1 Corinthians 5; Philippians 2:12-13). They did not tell them to wait for an apostle to be present in order to exercise direct authority, nor did they refer them to any other church authority, indeed they urged the churches to act themselves.

It could be argued that the situation among the churches in Asia, when the apostle John received the seven letters from the Lord of glory (Revelation 1-3), cried out for some external authority, if that was the way the Lord wanted to deal with their many problems. But each church is addressed separately and each church is required to apply the Lord's instructions under its own leadership. Enough time had elapsed after Pentecost for some synodical or other church structure to be advocated, or a 'bishop' to be appointed; but this was not the Lord's plan for the churches. Each was responsible directly to him.

The word 'church' or Ecclesia is used in the New Testament in three ways. It is sometimes used to indicate an assembly of civic authorities (Acts 19:39). Its spiritual usage is confined either to the total company of the Lord's people — the elect (Hebrews 12:23) — or to a local group of these people (1 Corinthians 1:2). The word 'church' is never used to denote a group of churches in a geographical area, e.g. Church of England or in a denominational sense. e.g. the Methodist Church.

Local churches then are free from all external ecclesiastical authority, but this does not mean they bear no relationship to each other.

Questions

1   It has been said you can prove any system of church order from Scripture. Is this true?
2   Does independency exclude a church asking for or accepting help from other churches or from an 'association'?

3.
Co-operation among churches

The New Testament requires that local churches should seek to express their unity in Christ by practical inter-dependence, working with each other while not losing their independence.

The local churches in the New Testament co-operated in evangelism, and charitable projects. Their working together in evangelism can be seen in the Jerusalem church sending Barnabas to help at Antioch (Acts 11:22-24), in the sending of Timothy by the Lystra church to work with Paul (Acts 16:1-3 compared with 1 Timothy 4:14), and the sharing of resources of man power and money for the advance of the Gospel (Acts 20:4; Philippians 4:14-16). Their co-operation in charitable projects is reflected in the collection arranged by Paul for the poor believers in Jerusalem (Acts 11:27-30; 2 Corinthians 8 and 9). When they worked together they were still independent churches and no decision could be made by some other body that was binding upon them, unless they agreed it should be so.

Co-operation in inter-church discipline and clarification of understanding of Christian doctrine is seen in the meeting at Jerusalem of representatives of the Antioch church with the apostles and the elders and members of the Jerusalem church, recorded in Acts 15:1-16:5. This is sometimes called the Council of Jerusalem and is used as a proof that local churches should come under the control of inter-church councils or synods; but this argues too much from too little. There was good reason for little Antioch taking big Jerusalem to task even though, as it turned out, the latter was innocent. Jerusalem did not send the false teachers about whom Antioch complained. However, the occasion was used to underline the great doctrine of justification by faith only, and the decisions reached carried apostolic authority.

I believe when elders from local churches meet for prayer and consultation, and they believe the Lord has spoken to them on a particular issue, then the local churches to which they return should give special respect to what those elders decide. The local churches are not in any way bound by such decisions but it would be foolish for them to be rejected simply on the grounds that they came from a group meeting apart from the local churches themselves. Those churches should give due weight to what the gathered elders believed was from the Lord. None of this alters the basic position that local churches under Christ are free to act as they believe he is directing them in the Scriptures, and by his Spirit. Jack Hoad writes in *The Baptist,* page 227:

> When bible-ruled baptists speak of 'an association' or 'a convention' of churches, they retain in the fullest sense the local independence of the local churches and are expressing the plurality of such churches in any stated area, as the scriptures do in Acts 9:31; Philippians 3:6 and 1 Timothy 3:15.

A note to this is appended on page 313:

> If the alternative reading in the singular of the word church in Acts 9:31 is insisted upon, then the baptist understands this to be the collective noun expressing plurality, plus an acknowledgement of the common likeness; that is, all are independent churches of Christ.

Co-operation among New Testament churches was largely made possible by the activities of the apostles. This gives rise to the questions, Are there apostles today? Are modern bishops direct descendants of the apostles?

There is convincing evidence to prove there cannot be an apostolic succession nor a position of an apostle in churches today. One qualification of an apostle was that he had seen the risen Christ (Acts 1:21-22; 1 Corinthians 9:1), and another was the ability to perform miracles (2 Corinthians 12:12). No one nowadays has these qualifications. Also, Paul tells us in Ephesians 2:20 that the church is built on the foundation of the apostles and prophets. We cannot lay the foundation of the church again. It is laid once and for all.

The apostles laid down the truth to be received. They received this from the Lord himself (Luke 24:45-47; John 16:12-15; Galatians 1:11-16) and their teaching is recorded in the Scriptures. The converts on the day of Pentecost continued in the apostles' teaching (Acts 2:42) and that must be our position still. The only apostolic succession is in the Scriptures and in the continuing proclamation of the gospel throughout the world. In notes for a local Bible study John Benton has written:

> Although the Twelve are absolutely unique, the Church as a whole is apostolic as it continues the mission of Jesus in the world, following in his steps and preaching the 'tradition' or 'deposit' of truth passed down from the original apostles which has been once and for all entrusted to us (1 Timothy 6:20; 2 Timothy 1:14; Jude 3).
>
> In particular there is an ongoing gift of missionary preacher and church planter. This was an integral part of the work of the original apostles and unlike their revelatory function, is a continuing work (Romans 1:1,5,9,13,15).
>
> Present day inflated views of authority among churches are corrected by the New Testament. The true authority of the original twelve including Paul is to be seen only in terms of their being vehicles of divine revelation, not otherwise. It is the word of God, not the men, which is authoritative — hence the showdown between Peter and Paul in Galatians 2. Peter must act in accordance with the *gospel*.
>
> The continuing work of the apostle is the pioneer preacher and church planter. We still desperately need men with such a ministry today. He is the man who is gifted and empowered to go to barren regions and labour until 'the temple of God' has been founded in that area, and then when his work is done to pass humbly on like the father of an adult child. He is ever a friend to the church, ever ready to give counsel and advice should they ask. But he has no commanding authority over them other than the word of God.
>
> Having said that, if a group of churches or pastors find the ministry of some particular man or men of especial help to them so that they wish to benefit as a group from this man or

men and associate together around them, there is nothing illegitimate about that. We think of the Westminster Fellowship and the late Dr. Lloyd Jones. That kind of association together may be fine, though it would be wrong to call such a man an apostle. However, if such a man assumes a position, or is put in a position of authority over the churches and pastors, that is to depart from Scripture, it is to make the man into a pope. Christ alone is the head of the churches (Ephesians 1:22; 5:23).

Much of what we have said about apostles can also be said about prophets. The teaching of the prophets is in the Scriptures as the final revelation of God to us (Ephesians 2:20). There maybe a ministry in the churches today that can be called prophetic. But since the apostles and prophets were foundational no one should be called a prophet nor an apostle, nor should anyone presume to have prophetic or apostolic authority over local churches.

Questions

1   What degree of commitment, if any, should a church give to an 'association'?
2   In what circumstances should a church withdraw from an 'association'?

4.
Christ the Head of the body

Independent church life demands a high degree of spirituality. Without this any system of church order will fail, but this is especially true of independency. We have no structure outside a local church to prevent its collapse or decline into confusion. The life and survival of each church depends on the presence of the Lord (Matthew 18:20; Revelation 3:20). After Jesus Christ was raised from death he was given 'all authority in heaven and on earth' (Matthew 28:18; John 17:2), and the Father appointed him 'head over everything for the church' (Ephesians 1:22; 4:15; Colossians 1:18). No church or church committee can appoint a head of the church. This was God's prerogative, and he has not appointed any human person to have authority over his churches. He has set his dear Son in the seat of power and he has not delegated that authority to anyone else. Christ alone must rule in his kingdom and each local church (Revelation 1:12-20). He rules through the Scriptures and by the Holy Spirit who guides us into the truth and enables us to apply the truth to every situation.

In Scripture the headship of Christ is linked with the church seen as his body (Ephesians 1:22-23; 4:15-16; Colossians 1:18). We must understand that a church is not merely a club run in accordance with a set of rules laid down a long time ago. A church has only a right to the name if there is a vital spiritual connection with the living Lord, as our bodies have a living union with our heads. Our Lord's picture of the connection between a vine and its branches gives us the same teaching (John 15:1-8).

Both rule and life are involved. A church may hold the doctrine of the headship of Jesus Christ but if it is not submissive to his rule through the Scriptures the doctrine is meaningless. A church needs also to be vibrant with spiritual life, without this it is not a true church according to the New Testament. In practice there will be at least six signs of Christ being the head of a church as its ruler and life giver.

First, the whole church in all its parts and in all its activities will be much in prayer 'in the Spirit, on all occasions with all kinds of prayer and requests' (Ephesians 6:18).

Second, there will be regular exposition of the Word and a constant reference to the Scriptures in every discussion and in the making of every significant decision. We may talk a lot about the authority of Scripture but if we do not search the Scriptures for the direction of our church life and for guidance to solve the problems we face, then all our talk is in vain.

Third, there will be positive aspiration to holiness. In accordance with Peter's directive, 'As obedient children, do not conform to the evil desires you had when you lived in ignorance. But just as he who called you is holy, so be holy in all you do; for it is written: "Be holy, because I am holy"' (1 Peter 1:14-16). Such holiness is not harsh or forbidding but purity blended with love among the members. The church as a body will 'build itself up in love, as each part does its work' (Ephesians 4:16).

Fourth, there will be unity as the members recognise they depend on one another and as they work to strengthen each other in the faith. (1 Corinthians 12:14-27; Ephesians 4:15-16; Hebrews 10: 24-25).

Fifth, there will be direction. The Lord will be constantly moving the church forward in its understanding of and obedience to the truth, in its impact on the local community and in evangelistic enterprise at a personal, local, national and international level.

Sixth, there will be both order and liberty just as a healthy body is well structured and this makes possible free flowing and graceful movement. In local churches two extremes are possible. On the one hand the organisation can be too rigid and the structure so complicated as to stifle evangelistic enterprise, and a spontaneous flow of love and caring concern. The body is bound. On the other hand the structure can be so slack as to leave the church floundering like a poor body afflicted with cerebral paralysis. Too little organisation results in confusion, and to important work or certain groups of people being neglected. That can also lead to vacuums which are then filled by people who may be keen but not suitable, while those who are more suitable are left aside. There should be enough organisation to ensure the co-ordination of all the parts and avoid confusion; but structure is not to be so tight as to limit free flowing movement.

Leaders, therefore, must seek to ensure that the body is in good working order to stimulate growth and to prepare for work. Inefficiency leads to confusion and frustration and is dishonouring to the Lord. But a church should not be like an efficient machine that produces nothing or goes nowhere.

We are ready now to look more directly at the structure of local churches. How does the Lord, the Head of the church, in practice exercise his rule in a local church?

Questions

1 Does the leadership in your church allow too much individual enterprise or too little?
2 What direction is the Lord giving to your church at this time?

5.
Plurality of elders and deacons

Since the Second World War every part of life generally has been questioned, and churches too have been put under the scrutiny of Scripture. Our worship and fellowship, our evangelism and missionary enterprise have all been affected, as has church administration.

For example, in the earlier part of this century the most common structure in local churches was a pastor with a group of deacons. In the absence of a pastor the church secretary often became the leader; but now this arrangement is being seriously questioned and the most significant change has been towards a plurality of elders.

These changes have caused an upheaval in many churches, and troubled members have asked 'Were the people in the past so wrong? We respected them and the Lord blessed their ministry, how can it be that they were so wrong at this point?'

Such questions are understandable and we must always beware of change for change's sake, or simply to be in the fashion. The Lord blesses us despite our imperfections, and no generation has a complete understanding of any aspect of biblical truth. It is no disrespect to godly people in the past for us today to follow Scripture, wherever that leads us, for to do so is to submit to the Lord himself. In a paper 'The position of a pastor' Robin Dowling sets the biblical scene like this:

> The New Testament assumes that every church will have more than one (elder), and when the origins of church elders are examined, the evidence in support of a plurality is

overwhelming. Those same origins also teach us much regarding the qualifications and characteristics of elders.

In many societies there was, and in some still is, a system of administration centred on the elders of a local community.

The Jews carried this system with them into the dispersion. In some other places the communal approach had been superseded by government by council or committee, but respect for age persisted, and often the titles used were those derived during earlier ages. The title 'elder' was commonly used in many areas around the Mediterranean, and so it is not surprising that the Christian churches should adopt not only the system but also the title. There is no record of the institution of the eldership principle in the New Testament. There was no need for any specific instructions from Jesus or the apostles because the churches were intended to use the practices familiar to all. The only area which did need to be covered was that of qualification for office. The Jewish elders were responsible for administration and discipline, not worship; similarly the elders of other societies were not concerned with worship. The elders of the churches were very much concerned with it, as well as administration and discipline, and so the Pastoral Epistles make spiritual qualities an essential part of the requirements for office.

It can be seen that government of the churches by a plurality of elders was natural to the early Christians. In modern times virtually every organisation, every society, is ruled by a committee or council or body of some sort. Since the New Testament makes no provision for any alternative organisation then we have no warrant to use any other practice. The diaconate came into being to aid the eldership, not to replace or reduce it.

The adoption of a plurality of elders is in fact a return to the practice of at least some earlier Congregational and Baptist churches. For example, the 16th century baptist leader, John Smyth held that 'Christ hath set two sorts of ministers in his church: some who are called pastors, teachers or elders, who minister the word and sacraments, and others called deacons, men and women, whose ministry is to serve tables.'

William Kiffin in the 17th century 'was favoured with three

eminently able and gracious assistant ministers (or co-pastors, or joint elders as they were sometimes known)'. *(Stranger than fiction,* B.A.Ramsbottom, Gospel Standard Trust Publications.)

The puritan, John Owen wrote: 'There were many bishops in one city, in one particular church (Philippians 1,1)...Such bishops whereof there may be many in the same church, of the same order, equal in power and dignity with respect unto office.'

It is difficult to know why the practice fell out of use. Perhaps in a time of spiritual decline there were not suitable men in the churches, or maybe a trend to a 'professional' ministry squeezed out 'laymen'. But very often the deacons were able men and in practice exercised eldership gifts. Whatever the reasons for the decline of plural eldership it is interesting to read of C. H. Spurgeon's experience when he began his London ministry in 1854. He tells us:

> When I came to New Park Street, the church had deacons, but no elders; and I thought, from my study of the New Testament, that there should be both orders of officers. They are very useful when we can get them — the deacons to attend to all secular matters, and the elders to devote themselves to the spiritual part of the work; this division of labour supplies an outlet for two different sorts of talent, and allows two kinds of men to be serviceable to the church; and I am sure it is good to have two sets of brethren as officers, instead of one set who have to do everything, and who often become masters of the church, instead of the servants, as both deacons and elders should be.
>
> As there were no elders at New Park Street, when I read and expounded the passages in the New Testament referring to elders, I used to say, 'This is an order of Christian workers which appears to have dropped out of existence. In apostolic times, they had both deacons and elders, but, somehow, the church has departed from this early custom. We have one preaching elder — that is, the Pastor — and he is expected to perform all the duties of the eldership.' One and another of the members began to enquire of me, 'Ought not we, as a church, to have elders? Cannot we elect some of our brethren who are qualified to fill the office?' I answered that we had better not disturb the existing state of affairs, but some enthusiastic young men said that they would propose at the church-

meeting that elders should be appointed, and ultimately we did appoint them with the unanimous consent of the members. I did not force the question upon them; I only showed them that it was Scriptural, and then of course they wanted to carry it into effect.

(*The Full Harvest*, Vol.2, Page 74)

What is the biblical evidence that local churches should be led by a plurality of elders assisted by a body of deacons?

A comparison of Scripture with Scripture reveals that the terms pastor, elder and overseer (bishop in some versions) describe different aspects of the same ministry within the church (Acts 14:23; 20:17-28; Philippians 1:1; 1 Timothy 3:1-13; Titus 1:5-9; 1 Peter 5:1-4). The term pastor suggests shepherding and loving care in terms of teaching, counselling and correcting. Elder — indicates maturity in experience of life and in the application of Scripture to life. Overseer — suggests responsibility and authority though answerable to a higher authority.

Wherever in the New Testament these leaders are mentioned it is always in the context of local churches, and the reference is always to a group of elders or a group of deacons. There is never a suggestion that there would normally be only one elder or one deacon.

Questions

1   Is your church taught regularly about church order?
2   Is plurality of elders a matter of cultural setting, temperament, or biblical authority?

6.
Advantages of plural eldership

We should not treat these matters as of little concern to the health and progress of the church. The Scripture never gives us guidance without there being good and substantial reasons for it. We will see more of the importance of a plurality of leadership when we discuss the ministry of elders and deacons in more detail; but there is no doubt that without plurality in leadership churches are liable to be hemmed in to the limitations of one man. No one man has all the wisdom or all the gifts necessary for the all round growth of a local church.

Where there is a 'full-time' elder it is not surprising if his influence in the church is greater than the others. For this reason I believe that for plurality to be effective a 'full-time' elder needs, if possible, to have at least two other colleagues.

There is evidence of our heavenly Father's compassion here. The burdens of pastoral ministry are very great and many men have broken down under the weight of these burdens. The breakdown is sometimes physical, sometimes psychological and sometimes spiritual, or it may be a combination of these problems. The question 'Who pastors the pastor?' can in part be answered in terms of such things as personal fellowship, pastoral conferences and sabbaticals. But there is no doubt that the strength that comes from effective fellowship within the body of elders is the best on-going answer.

There are other practical reasons for a plurality of elders; John Benton has listed some of them:

1. Often there are many pastoral problems to deal with at the same time.

2. One man cannot be on call all the time, especially if he has a family to care for.

3. Different people in the church relate best to different personalities. It is wise to remember this when elders are being appointed. (But this can be turned to disadvantage if one man becomes disproportionately popular. This may be for good or for bad reasons, but either way the problem needs to be faced).

4. One man alone can become headstrong and wilful (3 John:9).

5. Also if one man leads the church it gives the impression that he is the head and so obscures the headship of Jesus Christ.

(Study notes prepared from Guildford Church).

I have to confess that for me plural eldership is a discipline. I am a decision maker by nature; I take the personal view that even a wrong decision is better than none at all. However, I am bound by Scripture and by the Lord whose ways are always best, and I have learned to thank him for the love and wisdom of fellow elders who have often saved me from my own folly. So the eldership is a group of godly men working together in the church for the good of the people and the glory of God.

'For waging war you need guidance, and for victory many advisers' (Proverbs 24:6).

Another important practical advantage in having a plural eldership is that it helps to cushion the effects of radical changes among the leaders. Where there is but one elder/pastor around whom the church revolves, everything tends to stop or at least to become erratic if that person should move away or die. This is a common experience. A church is built up to a certain point, the pastor leaves and the church goes back a few or many degrees. A new pastor is called and he has to work hard to bring the church back to where it was, before he can then take it further. A plural eldership is not an infallible answer to this problem but it can prevent the problem occuring or at least minimize its effects.

None of these things suggest that a church cannot be led or pastored unless there are a number of men with eldership gifts. In the early days of a fellowship one person alone may lead, but from the beginning it is well to work and pray for a group of elders with a variety of gifts and talents to pastor and oversee the church, and likewise for a group of deacons.

When a church is being founded or is very small one person may have to fulfil many functions and all kinds of chores will fall to him. The one man may play the musical instrument, give out the notices, look after the finances and at the same time endeavour to preach, teach and evangelise among people of all ages. Such people need the prayers and the practical help of other churches. It is very desirable that new work should be in the hands of two or more families rather than to be the responsibility of one family alone. From the beginning the biblical principles of plural ministry should be taught, and as soon as possible responsibilities should be shared as the Lord gives suitable people.

In a more developed situation before elders are appointed some duties can be delegated to deacons. When there is a plural eldership one man will not be expected to meet all the needs of pastoral ministry. Few men have all the gifts of teaching and preaching and evangelism. Most have predominantly one of these abilities. In a plural eldership there is greater possibility of preserving one man from the pressure of being expected to 'do it all'.

Questions

1   Would you or your pastor be willing to see the leadership of your church shared with other elders?
2   What hinders a plural eldership being established in your church?

7.
Responsibilities of elders

Elders are responsible to oversee the whole life of the church. In particular they must care for the spiritual needs of the members remembering that they will have to give account to God for their faithfulness in that ministry (Hebrews 13:17; 1 Timothy 3:5; Acts 20:28).

This work requires the exercise of a variety of gifts which ideally will be spread through the eldership. Each elder will have different gifts, talents and personality from the others, and each church will have a different mix of elders.

Some people believe that all elders are to be preachers. Dr. Peter Masters assesses this position:

> In a growing number of churches, for example, the minister has been greatly undermined by the brand new idea that the elders of the church are all entirely equal, and that all of them are preaching elders. This novel arrangement has come about in the last twenty years and has gained popularity, curiously enough, in both Reformed and charismatic circles.
>
> (*Sword and Trowel* 1985 No2 p.24).

I believe Dr. Masters is right in rejecting the notion that all elders are public preachers. Passages of Scripture used to support this notion are Acts 14:23; Ephesians 4:11-12; 2 Timothy 4:1-5; Hebrews 13:7 & 17. None of these texts deal with the subject at all, but we need to give closer attention to four others:

1 Timothy 3:2 where elders are to be 'able to teach', but as Dr. Masters says 'this by no means implies a preaching function. Public preaching is not necessarily in mind at all. Every overseer or shepherding elder will need to have an aptitude to teach which will be essential for personal counselling, Bible class work, and so forth.'

Titus 1:9. Once again it is clear that Paul does not have public preaching specifically in mind here. This may be included but the main idea is spiritual ministry on a personal level.

1 Peter 5:1-2; Acts 20:28. Shepherding may include public preaching but its main responsibility is nurturing, protecting and encouraging each member of the church.

Far from the New Testament insisting that all elders are to be public preachers there is one text (1 Timothy 5:17) that seems to be conclusive that while all elders are to 'direct the affairs of the church', some of them will concentrate on preaching and teaching. All elders are to minister to the people of God under their care. They are to be channels through which the Lord builds his church (Matthew 16:18). We can compare the three offices of Jesus Christ — prophet, priest and king — with the three descriptions given to leaders of local churches:

     prophet compared with elder,
     priest compared with shepherd,
     king compared with overseer.

These ministries were not separate in our Lord and they are not distinct among church leaders. There is a blending of the ministries, but all three aspects are to be exercised by the leaders as a whole.

First, there must be the teaching. Jesus Christ as prophet is the fountain of wisdom and he has channelled that wisdom to us in the Scriptures. Elders are to be men of wisdom. They are to have good understanding of the Scriptures and they are responsible to see that the church is given sound doctrine applied to every aspect of the lives of the members.

Second, the priestly function of dealing gently with those who are ignorant and are going astray (Hebrews 5:2 contrasted with Ezekiel 34:4-6) may be likened to pastoring or shepherding. Jesus Christ is the good shepherd who cares for his sheep even to the point of giving his life for them (John 10:14-15), and he is the chief shepherd (1 Peter 5:4). Elders are to be 'shepherds of the church of God' (Acts 20: 28-31), which means they are to keep 'an eye on' all the members, try to ensure they are protected from false teaching, false fears and from straying into unwisdom or ungodliness.

Third, our Lord is king (John 18:36-37; Revelation 19:16) and he rules as Head of his church. This rule of Christ is to be reflected in the elders as they oversee the church. They are to teach the word of God, and seek to bring the church into submission to the authority of Scripture. It is the duty of the elders to ensure that members are guided, that the wayward are corrected and the rebellious are disciplined according to the principles laid down in Scripture. The elders as a body are responsible for these things. They are together elders, pastors and overseers.

Questions

1 Are the ministries of prophet, priest and king being adequately catered for in your church?
2 Where they are not, what can be done about it?

8.
The position of elders

Our whole approach to the subject will depend on our starting point. Do we begin with the idea that there are 'offices' to be filled in local churches, or with the idea that the Lord gives gifts to be exercised within local churches? This distinction may not at first sight appear to be very significant. We may even feel there is no distinction, since we can put them together by saying that those with the appropriate spiritual gifts should be appointed to certain offices. This would be in harmony with the view of the puritan John Owen whose writings in this field are valuable and instructive.

However, the weakness of this position is that it borrows too much from the ecclesiastical structures of the Roman and Anglican churches. It ignores the fact that the term 'office' is nowhere to be found in the New Testament in this connection. It does appear in the Authorised Version in three places, but an examination of those texts will show that they import an idea that was not in Paul's mind.

Romans 11:13 'I magnify mine office'. The word is correctly translated 'ministry' in the New International Version. The apostle is not referring to an office he holds but to the work he does as an apostle.

Romans 12:4 'all members have not the same office'. The word here is better translated 'function'. The apostle is not saying there are different positions people hold in the church, but that they all do different things.

1 Timothy 3:1 'If a man desires the office of a bishop, he desireth a good work'. The New International Version translates this: 'If anyone sets his heart on being an overseer, he desires a noble task'.

In this case as W.E. Vine says, 'the word "office" has nothing to represent it in the original'.

The whole idea of people in a local church holding office with a job specification prescribed in advance is foreign to the New Testament. The emphasis is on the use of gifts and talents the Lord has given.

But is this important? I believe it is. The idea that there are offices in the churches to be filled has resulted in churches being determined to fill those offices even with people who are not suitably gifted. Also, there have grown up some fixed ideas as to what those offices are, and in many cases those fixed ideas have had little warrant in Scripture. A result has been that churches have looked for men to fill a fixed specification, and if in the event a man has failed to fulfil expectations, irritation or worse has occurred. Also these things have generally led to a neglect of the spiritual gifts given to people other than those 'called' to fill the 'office'.

When we turn back to Scripture we not only discover an absence of the whole notion of 'office', we also find an emphasis on spiritual gifts. It is true that there are people called deacons and people called elders. Does this mean there are those two offices? If it did we would be warranted in referring to 'Elder Black' or 'Deacon Smith', as we have called some men 'Pastor Carr' or 'Pastor Davies'. This is rather like calling Mr. Mack — Butcher Mack, or Mr. Donald — Carpenter Donald. We normally prefer to emphasise the talent rather than the trade, so we speak of Mr. Donald the butcher. In the same way the emphasis in Scripture on spiritual gifts leads us to speak of Mr. Quick the elder, or Mr. Silver the deacon.

Again, does this really matter? I believe it does. One important benefit is that men are not judged on their ability to fill a preconceived function, but on their exercise of a spiritual gift they had already given evidence of possessing.

A further result is that churches discover in their members the spiritual gifts the Lord has already given, and encourage the exercise of those gifts. It becomes possible for a much broader and more complete view of all the Lord intends for the church. We approach the problems then with a consideration of spiritual gifts the Lord has given rather than with a concern to fill an office with a predetermined specification.

This leads us to see that the whole church should be exercising spiritual gifts before considering the appointment of elders or deacons. In Scripture the whole church is involved in ministry at the physical and material level and at the spiritual level. The whole church should be a serving, ministering community. The importance of this order of things is that gifts emerge in their exercise and this provides the church with the evidence needed for the appointment of those who will specifically function as elders or deacons. Instead of the church suddenly requiring some kind of leader and seeking for such a person in a vacuum, the right person may already be obvious. Indeed perhaps the church should already have recognised the leadership gift without waiting for a 'vacancy' to be filled.

A further benefit will be that those appointed to specific positions of leadership will not be left to 'do it all'. The common unbiblical distinction between an hierarchy and laity is also eliminated. All church members have the same status in Christ, and he gives gifts to each according to his sovereign purpose. The gifts make no difference to status.

Although we reject any distinction between so-called 'laity' and 'clergy', we tend to perpetuate the distinction in practice. For example, we do so when we insist on an elder conducting a prayer meeting, a communion service or baptisms. It is natural that normally an elder will serve the church in these ways, but there is no biblical warrant for never using others. Certainly there is no special virtue belonging to those who conduct the Lord's Supper or believer's baptism giving those ordinances validity. They are made valid by the presence of Christ and the obedience of the church to his commands. We also perpetuate an unbiblical distinction between 'laity and clergy' when only elders ever pray or read the Scriptures in gatherings for worship.

The position of elders in a local church then is not that of people holding offices, but of people called to exercise spiritual gifts the Lord has given them.

Questions

1   Are there people in your church with gifts and talents which are not being used? What can be done about this?
2   Are your leaders expected to do things they are not gifted for? What can be done about this?

9.
Functions of the elders

We have laid down some basic principles about the position of elders, and now we must consider their functions in a little more detail. As we do so we need to beware of establishing a pattern and then 'setting it in concrete'. We have argued against this way of thinking. If we begin with the gifts and talents God has given rather than pre-conceived specifications, we will be open to flexibility. This means the allocation of work will be based first on the gifts and abilities of each elder. None will be compelled to attempt work for which he is unsuited. If the Lord has not given certain gifts to any of the leaders there are things that can be done. The church should pray for people with those gifts to be given. Meantime, the question is asked, if the Lord has not given the gifts does he not want the work to be done? The answer may be that this avenue of service is not necessary at this particular time. If the answer is that the work is vital and must be done, then someone can be asked to attempt the task, assured of the prayer support and understanding of the church. In these circumstances hidden abilities may be revealed or the Lord may give the talent needed.

The ideal is a perfect match between the needs of a church and the available leadership gifts. One way of viewing the needs an eldership must try to cover, is to liken the church to its building. The numbers on the diagram represent:

1. People coming toward the church as a result of evangelism, growth in families and people moving into the area. Here the gifts needed are for evangelism, evangelistic literature production, counselling enquirers (individually or in groups), counselling young families.

2. People newly converted.
Here the gifts are to prepare people for baptism and church membership, and nurturing in the early days of the Christian life.

3. The main body of the church.
Here the gifts needed are teaching and preaching, visiting and pastoring people of all ages; leading worship; oversight of all groups, library, bookstall, music and church meetings.

4. Missionary support and the sending of people for work in other parts of the United Kingdom and the world.
Among other things the gift of encouragement is needed here.

5. People on the way out from the church because of backsliding, discipline, disaffection or simply moving to another town.
Here patience with difficult people and an understanding of moral and social problems are desirable.

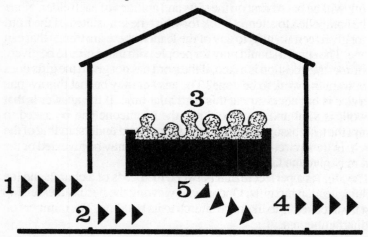

1. People coming toward the church
2. Newly converted people
3. Established membership
4. Missionary thrust
5. On the way out

However any eldership decides to divide up the work, this analysis shows up the main areas to be considered. There must always be objectives and in Ephesians 4:11-13 Paul tells us what the main objectives are. First he says that pastors and leaders are 'to prepare God's people for works of service so that the body of Christ may be built up'. This means they are to train the whole membership in the work. They will not do everything themselves but will use suitable people in the church as apprentices, training them for future leadership. The members are also to be encouraged and helped in their daily witness to the Lord among their friends and neighbours.

Elders must set an example of evangelistic zeal to the members. The elders should be active in their personal witness, and their prayers in the church should reflect a love for people who are separated from God and on the road to eternal ruin. Leaders will not be taken seriously when they urge members to be zealous in their daily witness for the Lord if they are not themselves good examples. Also they should encourage those in the church who have an ability to seek out and speak to unconverted people. All Christians have this responsibility but some are especially gifted in such work, and they should be trained and set apart for it.

It may be right for training courses to be arranged, or for members to be encouraged to go for training in counselling, leadership, children's and youth work, group leadership etc. The church is 'to build itself up in love as each part does its work' (Ephesians 4:16) and it is the duty of the elders to make this process possible.

The second objective is underlined by Paul in the words 'until we all reach unity in the faith and in the knowledge of the Son of God and become mature, attaining to the whole measure of the fulness of Christ'. This means helping each member to grow in love, in faith, in holiness, and in Christlikeness, and preparing them for entry into everlasting glory. This aim is to be achieved by teaching, personal counselling, and by developing effective spiritual fellowship among the members.

Elders must lead the church and in order to do this they need to give time for prayer and meditation, to assessing the work as a whole, and planning the direction and long term future of the church.

Some churches have discovered that the establishing of plural elders and deacons tends to rob the week to week activities of capable workers. The elders and deacons see more and more possibilities for the benefit of the church in the development of their

ministries. This is turn absorbs all their available time. They may
have been leaders in Sunday school and youth work, and now those
groups are deprived of their help. There are no easy answers, we
need to be realistic. No church can fill all its ministries to the full;
it may be necessary for elders and deacons to maintain their
involvement in other work for which they are suited until additional
capable help is available. This may mean their work as elders or
deacons suffers, especially if they also have their own families to
care for. There must be prayerful understanding of these situations
by the whole church. It is good to have an ideal church in our minds,
but the idealism of one person can be the cause of a breakdown in
another. We must use our 'renewed minds' (Romans 12: 1-2) in all
these things.

How long should elders serve the church? Should they retire? There
is certainly no warrant in the New Testament for an elder to be retired
at a certain age. Such a ruling can only be justified when elders are
thought of as holding an office, and we can then speak of a 'term of
office'. Eldership is a ministry and so long as a man is capable of
exercising that ministry he is still God's gift to the church. However,
as his powers wane by virtue of increasing age or ill-health, he should
gradually be released from responsibility. This principle is most easily
worked out in a situation of plural eldership in which other elders can
gradually take over the work previously done by the ageing brother.
However, problems arise where there is a dominance of one man, and
he continues to preach long after his powers have begun to decline.
Often the church he has been instrumental in building up now begins
to lose ground. If the man has been the preacher over many years, when
he does retire or die, often the effect on the church is devastating and
others have to begin to build all over again. I personally was so
concerned not to become an impediment to the Lord's work that I
retired at the age of 65 years. I felt I had some biblical support for this
in Numbers 8:25! Now I am under the guidance of others to use me so
long as they think it right before the Lord.

There are no rules about the length of time a preaching elder
should continue a ministry in one church. Many factors impinge on
this, the gifts and abilities of the man, the state of the church, and the
relationship between the man and the church. Short ministries are
not generally very constructive. I find it difficult to believe that a
man can do a worthwhile job in under five years, but some men seem
to run out of steam by then.

A preaching elder should not move to another church simply because he 'feels called'. His own aspirations and the Lord's dealings with the other church may indicate a change, but very careful thought needs to be given to the effects on a church when a preaching elder feels he must go elsewhere. The church itself must be given the opportunity to express its view along with full discussion among the leaders of both churches. A unilateral decision on the part of the pastor is very unwise. All concerned need to be submissive to the Lord and much prayer is needed along with heart searching.

Sometimes a church may need to relieve an elder of his responsibilities. Reasons for such action could be failure to fulfil his ministry, spiritual decline, lack of love for the church, pastoral insensitivity, departure from true doctrine, moral lapse or a serious decline in meeting the biblical qualifications of an elder. When an elder is accused of some fault or misconduct there must be care to deal with the matter honestly, with no cover up. But at the same time an elder must be protected from mischievous gossip and malicious slander. 'Do not entertain an accusation against an elder unless it is brought by two or three witnesses', and we might add 'reliable witnesses'. But also 'those who sin are to be rebuked publicly so that others may be warned' (1 Timothy 5:19-20).

On the other hand, an elder may feel it necessary to lay down his responsibilities for a number of reasons. He may think his circumstances are a hindrance, or that he is no longer able to do the work well. A lack of blessing in the church may cause him to be discouraged. The people may no longer be supporting him, or there may even be opposition to his ministry. But none of these things should be allowed to cause a man to resign without consultation with his fellow leaders.

Questions

1 Are certain kinds of people not being ministered to in your church?

2 In your church are new Christians adequately prepared for church membership?

10.
Parity of elders

Here we must deal with the question of whether a teaching elder (or elders) has some form of higher authority or leadership than the others. It is absolutely vital that this issue is clearly understood and a decision reached about it before any appointments are made. The decision is important for the life of the church; a wrong decision will be less than the best, but no decision at all leads to disaster. We must first consider two opposite positions and then ask if it is necessary to adopt either of them.

Arguments for a special status for teaching elders

In his very helpful book *God's plan for the local church* (Grace Publications) Nigel Lacey says: 'Some churches have appointed several elders and have declared that the minister of God's word is just one of this group ... This is wrong, we should have such a high esteem for the Word of God that we highly honour the office of the pastor and teacher.' He goes on to allow for more than one person preaching and teaching in a local church.

Dr. Masters argues:

> A new generation of church constitutions insist that the elders rule in absolute 'parity'. The unique role of a pastor as the presiding and preaching elder is swept away by this arrangement (though happily, some congregations continue to clothe the full-time elder with the more biblical status of

'pastor' because the members have not really understood the new system!).

We must make it clear that this modern system is quite different from the traditional Reformed position which recognises three kinds of officer; (1) the minister or pastor as the preaching elder. (In larger churches there could be more than one.) (2) the ruling elders. These are assisting, shepherding elders exercising a ministry of teaching and counselling other than the public ministry of the Word, and sharing the work of discipline and care with their pastor, who is the presiding elder. (3) Deacons. This is the viewpoint adopted by the Reformed tradition historically and is the position held by our Presbyterian brethren.

(Sword and Trowel 1985 No.2 pp.24, 25)

Dr. Masters believes that the apostle Paul's example is a pattern for us to follow today. He quotes 1 Corinthians 4:16-17; 11:2; 2 Thessalonians 2:15; John 14:26, and reasons:

It is a matter of the greatest importance that we defend the distinctive office and work of the preaching ministry because the efficiency of the leadership is at stake, and the system of the New Testament must not be tampered with. If God has established a system, then there is good reason for it.

The whole-time preachers of New Testament times, with their special leadership role, achieved mighty things by the grace and power of God. They were the senior men, and they were elders of a unique kind, but they badly needed the support of other elders, and deacons, otherwise God would not have ordained that these should be appointed.

Certainly the preaching elder was not an autocrat; a law unto himself. He was a teaching-shepherd, who presided over the other shepherds of the flock in such a way as to respect their God-given commission also.

These other officers were vital to the health and training of the churches, and essential to keep up the tempo of the work. They brought a range of abilities which the pastor lacked, which were exercised under his 'presidency'. The pastor-preachers needed their counsels and sometimes doubtless their restraint, for all men are subject to many temptations and weaknesses.

However, if the supporting or non-preaching elders (or the deacons, come to that) had decided to act as fellow-pastors, the system would have collapsed immediately.

Sadly, in our day, the distinctions between the preaching elder and the ruling (or shepherding) elder is being very badly blurred, and many problems are resulting.

(ibid. p.26)

Another very powerful argument for the special place of a preaching elder is based on the complete authority of the Word of God in the life of the church (as we have seen from Nigel Lacey). If this authority is to be exercised then those who teach and preach the Word must have a special role above the other elders, normally called ruling elders. Proof texts for this position are 1 Timothy 5:17; 1 Corinthians 9:9 & 14, and others where the word 'ministry' appears in the Authorised Version, Colossians 4:17; 1 Timothy 1:12; 2 Timothy 4:5. Also the 'angels' of the churches in Revelation 2 and 3 are assumed to be preachers or pastors commissioned by God to declare his word to those churches.

A further argument is that pastors have a special call from the Lord to teach and preach the Word, as did the apostles, and this call puts them in a special position of leadership among the elders.

Arguments for parity in the eldership

The word 'parity' is preferred to 'equality' because while there is a parity of position or responsibility among the elders, there is not equality in the sense that all have the same gifts and abilities.

These works of teaching and ruling may be distinct in several officers, namely, teachers and rulers; but to divide them in the same office of pastors, that some should feed by teaching only but have no right to rule by virtue of their office, and some should attend in exercise unto rule only, not esteeming themselves obliged to labour continually in feeding the flock, is almost to overthrow the office of Christ's designation, and to set up two in the room of it, of men's own projection.

(John Owen, Vol.16, page 48).

Those who hold this view believe it is wrong to take the special place of the apostles and their assistants as our pattern. Their position was a special one in the foundational days of the churches. Robin Dowling writes:

> It is important to note that the appointments of Timothy and Titus themselves do not give us any precedent for the appointment of elders ... because they were not 'called' by the churches, but were placed in the churches by an apostle ... We must always be careful not to read into the Scriptures traditions which we have adopted. Let the Scriptures speak for themselves. In regard to the Pastoral Epistles, there is a danger that the characteristics of the ministries of Timothy and Titus will be seen as appropriate for our pastors, whereas we should be studying the characteristics of those whom they appointed.
>
> (Paper *The position of a Pastor* - page 3)

The use of the word 'ministry' in the Authorised Version has misled many into using it to describe the work of full-time pastors calling them ministers. But this word is scattered throughout the New Testament not only in connection with the 'ministry of the Word' (Acts 6:4), but also in reference to domestic duties (Luke 10:40), handling finances (Acts 6:1; 11:29), mutual help (Romans 12:7; 1 Corinthians 12:5), preaching (Acts 6:4). The pattern in the New Testament is of ministering churches, all the members ministering in all kinds of ways to each other. Therefore texts that speak of an apostle's 'ministry' do not prove a special position for a 'minister' in the sense of a preaching elder.

All agree that the authority in a local church is Christ himself and his Word. This is absolute: but far and away from this giving anyone a special position, it is a warning against it, because to do so is to be in danger of ascribing infallibility to the preacher. The whole church, elders included, is to submit to the authority of the Word.

When the preacher has expounded the Word all the elders are responsible to ensure that it is applied to the life of the church and to all the members. We have been misled by the Authorised Version's use of the word 'office' — as we have seen in chapter eight. There is no such thing in the New Testament as a special 'ministry' or 'office' — the emphasis is on the use of gifts the ascended Lord has given to his church.

The 'proof texts' quoted in favour of a special role of preaching elders leave the matter very open indeed. The main one is 1 Timothy 5:17: 'The elders who direct the affairs of the church well are worthy of double honour, especially those whose work is in preaching and teaching'. As we have seen this verse completely shatters the notion that all elders are preachers and teachers, but does it put preaching elders in some sense above the others? The double honour refers to financial support as verse 18 makes clear: 'For the Scripture says, "Do not muzzle the ox while it is treading out the grain" and "the worker deserves his wages"'. Paying a man gives him extra time for work in the church, but does not raise him in rank above other elders. The most that can be argued is that there were differing ministries among the elders. The word 'especially' is a very strong one as Dr. Peter Masters points out: 'It means chiefly, mostly, particularly, or most of all. It is as strong a word as it could be'. This emphasises the special place that preaching and teaching must have in the life of the church. Without this it is doubtful if a church exists in the New Testament sense. But it does not prove that the preaching elders themselves have some kind of status above the others.

Any argument from the 'angels' in Revelation 2 and 3 is inconclusive. There have been many ideas as to who these angels are and it is claiming far too much to suggest that they are obviously preaching elders.

In this book I advocate a parity among the elders. Certainly the system of the New Testament must not be tampered with, and if God has established a system there is good reason for it but it is surely claiming too much to say that one or other position we have discussed is the New Testament system, and that to depart from either is to depart from Scripture. I believe the arguments for parity are more persuasive and that parity makes better provision for safeguards from abuse and benefits the churches as a whole. However, many of the principles of leadership, of the relationships between leaders, and between them and the members which we go on to discuss apply as much to those who take a different view on this particular point.

Questions

1 Given a plural eldership in your church, is there a clear understanding whether the elders have equal standing, or if one is above the others?
2 Why is it important that this issue is settled one way or the other and understood by the whole church?

11.
A 'call'

Many people speak of a 'call to the ministry'. By this they mean that they have received a special command from God to preach. The command is given in different ways; it may be an impression on the mind and heart during a time of prayer, reading the Scriptures or listening to a sermon. Sometimes this impression is received suddenly and unexpectedly. At other times it is a gradual pressure on the conscience that this is the will of God, and then a Scripture is given to confirm the 'call'.

To question such experiences will be surprising and even objectionable to some people, so I hope a personal testimony will encourage you to read on. From the age of ten I was often asked the usual question 'What are you going to do when you grow up?' My normal reply was, 'I don't know.' If I had dared to be honest I would have said, 'I think one day I will be a preacher.' This feeling became gradually more persistent until in the mysterious providence of God I found myself in Bible College. At the end of the course an invitation was received to become the pastor of the church at Cransford in Suffolk. It was then that the Lord gave me a Scripture to confirm that I should accept the invitation.

So why do I put 'call to the ministry' in quotation marks and question the concept which this implies? I do not mean to reject the Lord's leadings to me or to others, but to face real problems in this area arising from a wrong understanding and use of this kind of experience. Problems arise because men become so convinced of their 'call' that they become bitter and disillusioned when they are not invited to join an eldership or to become a pastor; or a church does invite them but the result is a disaster, and they blame the church or other factors when all the time the mistake is their own. It is very easy for us to deceive ourselves with our own inclinations, the misuse of Scripture, failure rightly to evaluate ourselves and our gifts, and by misunderstanding the Lord's dealings with us.

Another pitfall into which many have fallen appears when a man seeks the recommendation of his church to go to a Bible College, or accepts preaching engagements with a view to an invitation to a 'pastorate'. The man tells the church of his 'call' and the church says 'Well, if he's had a call what can we say? We mustn't stand in his way.' So the man is encouraged to proceed without serious biblical screening. This can work the opposite way also. A church may refuse for unworthy reasons such as jealousy or an unwillingness to lose a useful worker to encourage a man, who gives true evidence of a gift to preach. Or the church may demand evidence of an inward 'call' which the man cannot give though he may have every evidence of the appropriate gifts.

I believe another misuse of the inner feelings of a 'call' is the tendency for a man in a difficult situation to say, 'If I were not certain of my call I would have given up long ago, I could not go on'. This argument has given nerve to many a Christian worker and I would not wish to undermine the confidence of any hard-pressed servant of Christ. But I am convinced that even more solid ground for confidence and encouragement to persevere is to be found in God himself and in his promises (Isaiah 43:1-2; Matthew 28:18-20; Hebrews 13:5-6).

Satan is very easily able to convince us that we were mistaken after all in the 'call' no matter how sure we may have been up to the point. It is also true of course, that Satan can undermine our confidence in the Lord himself. But whereas 'the call' is not ultimately proveable, God's power and faithfulness are written large throughout the whole of the Scriptures. It is in him we must trust.

No system can prevent mistakes or even terrible disasters but the problems I have mentioned compel us to ask whether our understanding of the idea of a 'call' is well-grounded in Scripture. I believe it is a mistake to use the apostles and their actions in appointing leaders and elders as a pattern for the appointment of elders today. Paul was 'called to be an apostle' (Romans 1:1; 1 Corinthians 1:1). He was not chosen by a church; God equipped and appointed him apart from any human involvement (Galatians 1:15-17). Are we right to use this example for ourselves today?

Robin Dowling writes:

> The word 'call' is sometimes used to speak of a strong inward sense of vocation coupled with the outward ordering of circumstances by God. This is taken to be God's normal way of leading people into ministry and mission — although, in fairness, the involvement of the church in all this is not usually denied.
>
> However, this is not a biblical use of the word 'call'. The word 'call' is used theologically in the Scriptures in two main ways. It is used of the outward call of the gospel by which all are invited to receive God's salvation through repentance and faith (Matthew 22:1-14). It is also used to speak of the inward call of grace by which some are enabled to respond to the outward call (Romans 8:28-30). Now the verb 'to call' is used a few times in connection with ministry and mission always with reference to the apostle Paul. (Romans 1:1; 1 Corinthians 1:1; Acts 13:2; Acts 16:10). Study of these examples shows that the word 'call' in this sort of context always has to do with an external, supernatural occurrence. In the case of Acts 13:2 we find the Holy Spirit saying at Antioch, 'Set apart for me Barnabas and Saul for the work to which I have called them.' The Holy Spirit spoke, either in an audible voice or through one of the prophets referred to in Acts 13:1. Furthermore such 'callings' were not God's normal way of leading believers into ministry and mission but occurred at key points in the unfolding of God's saving process. The use of the word 'call' then to speak of a strong inward impression as God's normal method of leading people into ministry and mission must be questioned.
>
> Instead, the New Testament emphasises the appointment of men to pastoral ministry through the recognition by the church of certain qualifications (i.e. gifts and spiritual-human qualities) in those men. Guidelines about this are given in 1 Timothy 3:1-7 and Titus 1:5-9 (and reflected in 1 Peter 5:1-4). The normative nature of these guidelines is implied in the phrase 'the overseer must be...' The prospective pastor (i.e. overseer or elder) is not passive in all this. He will be a person

who aspires to and desires such work (1 Timothy 3:1), and will consequently have some awareness of his gifts and potential. However, just as the church, in Acts 6, chose 'seven men' with certain known qualities, so it is the responsibility of the local church to ascertain whether a person has the qualifications for pastoral ministry in that church.

(*Grace* Magazine, November 1984)

There is a view that says 'once a pastor, always a pastor'. A man has a 'call' and no matter whether he is actually functioning as a pastor/elder or not, he is still 'Pastor Pond'. This is a hangover from ecclesiastical traditions in which laity and clergy are separated and a 'reverend' is always a 'reverend'. I believe a man is only an elder in so far that he has been called by a church to exercise a pastoral ministry in that church, and is continuing to do so. The whole notion of a man being 'ordained' by a college apart from a local church, and then sometime later being assigned to a church or called by a church seems to me to be indefensible.

A man may believe in his heart that the Lord is equipping him for eldership ministry of some kind but until a church also believes that, he should beware of self-deception. He may not be deceived, but many men have lost their way and their families have suffered because they have come to a decision about themselves before a church has called them.

Questions

1   How can someone claiming a personal call to eldership be tested and by whom?
2   How can a feeling of an 'inward personal call' prove to be deceptive?

12.
Authority and leadership

In many churches a crisis of authority has arisen, and there have been a number of reasons for this. Teaching elders, holding the view that they have a special status have attempted to rule fellow elders in the church in an autocratic way. At the other extreme, when a plural eldership has been established, elders have also become authoritarian and in some cases they have tried to rule the preaching elder!

Then in some churches, where there has been a move away from the process of democratic decision making, elders have made the decisions rather than the church meeting. Rule by a majority vote has been exchanged for rule by elders! In some cases voting has been abandoned altogether.

Often the church has not clearly understood what is happening and the reasons for it. I know from experience that it is possible to teach these things over a long period and then for confusion still to arise when they are put into practice. Only when members see the arrangement working do they truly understand, and then they may decide they don't like what they see!

We cannot say too dogmatically that all authority in the local church resides in Jesus Christ, and that he exercises his authority through the Word and by his Spirit. All Christians equally have access to this one source of authority. Men are chosen to be elders because among other things they are recognised to be knowledgeable in the Scriptures, but this does not endow them with some new authority; they have none apart from the Word itself.

The word *exousia* (authority) in the New Testament is never used of elders. It was used of Jesus (Matthew 9:6; 28:18; John 17:2), of earthly powers (John 19:10; Romans 13:1-3), and it was used by Paul of the authority he had from Christ for the building up of believers, (2 Corinthians 10:8; 13:10). This word does appear in our translations of Hebrews 13:17 but there is no Greek word to warrant it; the Greek literally is 'obey your leaders and be submissive'. Nevertheless, the New Testament does provide for strong leadership on the part of the elders. This is implied in all three aspects of their work — eldership, pastoring and oversight. Paul instructs the Thessalonian believers to 'respect those who work hard among you, who are over you in the Lord, and who admonish you' (1 Thessalonians 5:12).

In 1 Timothy 3:5 Paul writes: 'If anyone does not know how to manage his own family, how can he take care of God's church?' Also in 1 Timothy 5:17 elders are to be those who 'direct the church' which is literally 'who take the lead'. In Hebrews 13:7 the writer refers to leaders and in verse 17 those leaders are to be obeyed; they are generally thought to be elders and their responsibility is placed in a very serious light. 'They keep watch over you as men who must give an account.' Such a work could only be fulfilled if their leadership is acknowledged.

Those who hold the view that there is parity of responsibility among elders must take seriously the problems of leadership that have arisen. Perhaps the main problem is highlighted by Dr. Peter Masters:

> Yet another problem is that of the 'committee syndrome'. The intention of Scripture (and here we note the tone of all Paul's instructions to Timothy) is that the resident preacher should keep the church on its toes spiritually. He bears the ultimate responsibility before God for ensuring that the people are inspired by the truth, challenged, encouraged, and exhorted to keep up their prayerful enthusiasm for the Saviour's work.
>
> He must answer to God if elders have been allowed to become complacent, or if the activities of the church have gradually run down. He will be finally answerable if nothing new has been attempted to gather-in souls and raise the Lord's standard in that place.
>
> The equal-elder system, like a committee with a 'rotational' chairman, is a negation of the whole notion of

leadership. C.H. Spurgeon so aptly remarked that if ten grooms were appointed to look after a horse, it would probably starve! If all elders are equal, who is to be the linchpin? Who will accept the ultimate charge from the Lord, expressed in the solemn, weighty second-person-singular as it was to Timothy and Titus?

Too many churches languish for want of a zealous and committed pastor who will make himself finally responsible for any lack of obedience and action on the part of the church. But the cosy mutuality of the 'equal elders' system is making matters worse than ever, because the pastor is no longer even nominally responsible to preside.

(Sword and Trowel, 1985 No.2 p.27)

While I do not think these problems destroy the idea of parity among elders, the difficulties that they raise must be taken seriously. Churches need to be led, and the leadership needs to be clear. People do not normally respond to a committee; because of this some churches have labelled their full-time preacher 'pastor' and he has become the focal point of the church's life. This is understandable when we remember that a full-time elder is normally a preaching elder, because of the demands of prayer, study and preparation involved in a preaching ministry. But the full-time preacher may not be the best leader, often he is not; he is forced into a role for which he is not suited. This is especially irritating when in certain areas others are more capable of leading, for example the conducting of church meetings.

The better way, more in harmony with the tone of Scripture, is for gifts to be recognised. Within the eldership there will be a variety of gifts and it is best for a gift of leadership to be recognised and allowed its head. There is to be a clear provision in the eldership for the particular work of teaching and preaching, and Acts 6:1-6 gives us the clue that those committed to this work should be allowed to make it their priority. There is no Scriptural warrant for saying that such preaching elders should bear more responsibility than other elders or deacons, rather that they should be relieved as far as possible. In fact this suggests that the leadership may best be in the hands of ruling elders who are not set apart to preach. But I am arguing for flexibility and for each eldership to develop its own manner of leadership. As the church changes and the eldership changes so the structure should also change. The great thing is for the church to be clearly led and for the various aspects of the work to be done by those best suited.

The members of the church need to know to whom to turn for information or help, or else confusion will arise. This should not be difficult to ensure but it can be neglected. Let the elders imagine that they are the least prominent member of the church, and then make sure that such a person would know and easily understand what is happening.

The church is not a democracy, it is a Christocracy. For this reason 'the church seeks not merely to discover the opinion of the majority of the members but rather through prayer and fellowship to know the mind of the Lord' (*We Believe,* page 30). This is a very practical matter. A democratic procedure fails to take account of the fact that the church is made up of members with varying degrees of understanding and experience. Take the matter of the appointment of elders or deacons. It is not unknown for unscrupulous or even well-meaning members to seek to influence less experienced members. In any case such decisions are too great a burden for new young members to bear.

Another failing of a democratic procedure is that it takes for granted that people may abstain or vote against what is proposed. This leads to division and hardening of positions. We will discuss procedures later in chapter 22 but for the moment let us say that the aim of the eldership will be to seek the unanimity of the church. The question remains as to how the elders are to exercise their leadership.

Do they make decisions without discussing the issues with the church? Do they (as some have done) discipline members who dare to question their decisions, recommendations or directions on the basis that such members are rebellious?

The spirit in which leadership is exercised, and the atmosphere of church decision making is vitally important. Our Lord taught that leaders are to be servants (Mark 9:33-35). The apostle Paul was concerned not to 'lord it' over others (2 Corinthians 1,24; and 13:10; 1 Corinthians 2:1-5) and the apostle Peter taught that elders were to be 'eager to serve' their members (1 Peter 5:1-4). Even in 1 Timothy 3:5 where Paul speaks of elders being able to 'manage' their own families he does not carry over the same word into the church context, rather he modifies the concept by saying 'how can he take care of God's church?' The words of Jesus must be etched into the

minds of every church leader: 'You know that the rulers of the
Gentiles lord it over them, and their high officials exercise authority
over them. Not so with you. Instead whoever wants to be great
among you must be your servant, and whoever wants to be first must
be your slave — just as the Son of Man did not come to be served
but to serve and to give his life a ransom for many' (Matthew 20:25-
28). And, remember, these words were addressed to apostles. If
apostles must be slaves, then elders cannot escape the challenge.

Paul presents us with the same challenge in Ephesians 5:21:
'Submit to one another out of reverence for Christ.' Elders are
members of the church and they are not exempt from the duty to
submit to their fellow members. Difficult as the concept may seem,
their leadership must be exercised in a spirit of submission. Paul
certainly worked this out both in the context of evangelism:
'Though I am free and belong to no man, I make myself a slave to
everyone, to win as many as possible' (1 Corinthians 9:19), and in
the context of a church: 'We do not preach ourselves but Jesus Christ
as Lord, and ourselves as your servants for Jesus' sake' (2
Corinthians 4:5).

In church life the submission of elders to members is not in terms
of 'the tail wagging the dog', rather it is in terms of service. For
example, elders submit to the needs of church members by recognising those needs and doing their best to satisfy them. Members
may appear to be difficult in not readily accepting their elders'
recommendations. Submission requires that elders patiently reason
with them. If members say 'we want more time to think and pray
over this matter', submissive elders will agree to such a request in
good grace. A member may be criticising the leadership about the
preaching. I know instances where an elder has been told he must
never mention a certain doctrine in his preaching. Where does
submission come in here? It comes, not in playing down unfashion-
able doctrine, but in the humility of the elder, his refusal to take
personal offence and in his willingness to spend time with the
member concerned. We fail to submit when we write people off as
being impossible to cope with.

Elders are to lead (Hebrews 13:17), which means they are
initiators and men of decision, but this is not with the authority of an
office, nor with an attitude of superiority but by godly example,
patient exhortation and humble service, to win the respect and
therefore the acceptance of the members. Elders need to remember

not only that they are 'building with bananas' (see Bibliography) but that they themselves bear the same characteristics.

An authoritarian approach is both unscriptural and dangerous. It undermines rather than reflects the headship of Christ, and it stifles spiritual growth because it tends to replace the personal access of a believer to the Word and the Spirit.

Some people reacting against slackness and indiscipline have practised 'heavy shepherding'. They have claimed the authority not only to demand strict adherence to Scripture, but also adherence to their directions in matters to which Scripture does not specifically speak, such as whom a person should marry, or whether to change a job. It is a pity that this has happened at a time when members have been more willing to consult elders for counsel and advice. Many have been discouraged from seeking such advice because of the spread of this authoritarian approach. Happy is the church where members feel free to share their problems and decision making with their elders in an atmosphere of love and understanding, which in no way undermines their own responsibility to the Lord and the universal priesthood of believers (1 Peter 2:9-10).

The answers to questions such as 'Who makes decisions, the members or the elders?' must be seen in the context of love, mutual submission and service. The elders must lead, or else the church will be confused. The elders must serve, or else their leadership will stifle the spiritual life of the church. Furthermore, these principles must be clearly understood by the church and all concerned before ever elders are appointed.

The idea of leadership being exercised by submission and service is not easy to comprehend and it is even more difficult to put into practice. The solution is found in reading over and over again the life of our Master himself. Paul reflected his Master's example when he likened his conduct to that of a nursing mother, 'we were gentle among you like a mother caring for her children. We loved you so much that we were delighted to share with you not only the gospel of God, but our lives as well, because you had become so dear to us' (1 Thessalonians 2:7-8). Could there be a clearer example of submission and service than the care of a mother for her baby? The baby's needs are priority, everything else has to be left when the cry is heard. Indeed, the mother's ear is tuned to the cry that others may not have heard.

But everything can be driven to extremes so we must note that in the same passage Paul says, 'You know that we dealt with each of you as a father deals with his own children, encouraging, comforting, and urging you to live lives worthy of God' (1 Thessalonians 2:11-12). Leadership therefore must bear the marks both of a nursing mother and of a wise father.

This principle of submission and service in leadership has been recognised by people in the business world. For example, Robert Greenleaf was director of management research with American Telephone and Telegraph, reputedly the world's largest corporation at that time. He wrote a book in 1977 entitled *Servant Leadership* in which he asserted that those who are leaders must serve those whom they lead and only those who serve are fit for leadership. Greenleaf offered this interesting test of good leadership:

> The best test, and difficult to administer is: Do those served grow as persons? Do they, while being served, become healthier, wiser, freer, more autonomous, more likely themselves to become servants?

When we understand leadership in this way we can also see how it harmonises with the biblical principle of the priesthood of all believers (1 Peter 2:9-10).

In a paper read at Emmanuel Bible College, Cebu, Philippines in 1984 Robert W. Ferris says:

> The assumption is simple, but far-reaching: people are valuable. Each human being is a creature of unique significance. Because of their uniqueness, not only with respect to one another but much more in contrast to everything else that exists, persons must always be viewed and related as persons, never as objects or things.

Ferris went on to show that servant leadership is a biblical necessity:

> On at least four occasions during the closing period of his earthly ministry, Jesus told his disciples 'if any one wants to be first, he must be the very last'. Do you suppose his purpose was to advise them how to get ahead in the kingdom of heaven? I am sure it was not! In fact, the disciples' quest to

get ahead, their aspiration to positions of prominence, was exactly the context which first elicited Jesus' remark. In this saying, rather, Jesus alerted them (and us) that the ethic of the kingdom inverts the depraved hierarchy of worldly values. The world tells us 'Be proud! Hold your head high. Let others know you are someone. Use your power to get ahead. Drive for the top. Aspire! Aspire! Aspire!' Jesus tells us, 'If anyone wants to be first, he must be the very last, and the servant of all' (Mark 9:35).

Sometimes a young man will find himself in a position of taking the lead among people older than himself. Paul's directions to young Timothy are very much to the point in this matter and a number of others. 'Do not rebuke an older man harshly, but exhort him as if he were your father. Treat younger men as brothers, older women as mothers and younger women as sisters with absolute purity' (1 Timothy 5:1-2).

Let us end this chapter with a few do's and don'ts for leaders generally.

1. Be careful of your own spirit. Pride will easily rear its ugly head in the form of dogmatism, arrogance or stand-offishness.
2. Don't 'do everything' because others cannot do the work as well as you. Encourage others to work even if it is not done so well as you would like.
3. Don't forge ahead dragging others reluctantly behind you.
4. Let other people get on with their work without you fussing. Find other ways of letting them know you are interested in them and of encouraging them.
5. Be sure your colleagues know what you expect of them. For example, at the close of a meeting where planning decisions are made, go over the items for action and make sure each person knows what he or she has been asked to do.
6. Beware of favouritism arising from family ties or special friendships. In the disagreement between Paul and Barnabas it is reasonable to assume that Barnabas was so keen to take John Mark because he was his near relation (Acts 15:36-41; Colossians 4:10).

Questions

1   How is the authority of Scripture applied in your church?
2   How could the leadership in your church be made more effective?

13.
The character and qualifications of elders

There must be submission to the Scriptures. A church member seeing in a dream a certain man, may believe this is the Lord's direction to a person who should be appointed an elder. This could be right, but the person seen in the dream must first be tested in the light of the solid requirements of Scripture. Some people think their 'hunches' are always right, but this is no substitute for patient diligent searching of the Scriptures.

The character of elders

There are two main Scriptures in which the qualifications of elders are specified — 1 Timothy 3:2-7 and Titus 1:6-9. Here is a brief survey of the requirements of elders set out in these two passages:
1. *'above reproach'* (1 Timothy 3:2). He must not give grounds for accusations against his conduct. This means not only freedom from public scandal but freedom from suspicion. None of us can prevent malicious people inventing stories about us (see Daniel 6:4-5, 1 Peter 4:14-16, Mark 14: 55-56), but we have to do our best not to give an excuse for such gossip. There may be times when a man is not appointed an elder because, although he is totally innocent, the mud of scandal sticks too firmly on him.
2. *'the husband of but one wife'* (1 Timothy 3:2; Titus 1:6). This is primarily directed against polygamy but the assumption is that an elder will be happily married. This does not exclude the appointment of a man who is single as an elder. If however, there is but one elder in a church, care must be taken that a single man in that

situation has the help of mature ladies in the church. Perhaps here we have another benefit of plural eldership, though as far as I know an unsung one!

3. *'temperate '* (1 Timothy 3:2). This is freedom from the influence of strong drink. It does not necessarily imply total abstinence but it certainly means great moderation. In these days we could add freedom from the influence of harmful drugs. God cannot use a drunkard as an elder. The principle holds good for any legitimate appetite; an elder must be able to control it rather than it controlling him.

4. *'self-control'* (1 Timothy 3:2; Titus 1:8). This is translated 'sober' in the Authorised Version but 'discreet', 'sober-minded', 'sensible' in others. The meaning of the word used is sober-minded, not having one's opinions swayed by sudden impulses. The result will be a sober judgement on problems being considered. It will also mean not reacting hastily to a problem that suddenly occurs, reserving judgement and refusing to come to ill-considered conclusions.

5. *'respectable'* (1 Timothy 3:2). Good behaviour in the sense of being modest, courteous and orderly. An elder will not carelessly flout normally accepted standards of etiquette, or give offence by crude behaviour.

6. *'hospitable'* (1 Timothy 3:2; Titus 1:8). All believers are exhorted to be hospitable (Romans 12:13; Hebrews 13:2; 1 Peter 4:9; 2 Timothy 1:16) and elders must lead by example in this grace. It also implies the elder's home is a place of love and peace where visitors feel comfortable and where the Lord is not dishonoured.

7. *'able to teach'* (1 Timothy 3:2). This is not of necessity public preaching or teaching. A good commentary on it is Titus 1:9: 'He must hold firmly to the trustworthy message as it has been taught, so that he can encourage others by sound doctrine and refute those who oppose it.'

8. *'not given to drunkenness'* (1 Timothy 3:3; Titus 1:7). This is clearly linked with 'temperate' but the emphasis here is not so much on the influence of alcohol on the mind, but on time spent lingering over drink. An elder will not drink for the sake of it. He will not sit for long periods with a glass in his hand, and we could add, nor with a plate of food or a cup of tea before him.

9. *'not violent but gentle'* (1 Timothy 3:3; Titus 1:7). An elder is not to be given to either physical or verbal violence. If he is quick-tempered or threatening, people will be afraid of him and will not

seek his help or advice (Ephesians 4:31). In contrast, an elder will be gentle and patient, not easily angered (1 Corinthians 13:5; Colossians 1:11). He will be tender and kind as was our Lord Jesus Christ (Matthew 11:28-30).

There is a little more in the word Paul uses for 'gentle'. It implies patiently taking into account all the facts of a case and dealing with each person according to his or her specific situation. I believe if an elder is truly displaying this quality he will always be open to the charge of being unfair because he may very well deal with two apparently similar situations in entirely different ways. In the one case he may appear to be lenient while in the other people will think he is severe.

10. *'not quarrelsome'* (or not contentious) (1 Timothy 3:3). There are some people with a hyper-critical spirit, always ready to see the worst in others or to pick a quarrel (Galatians 5:15). Such a man would achieve the opposite to the aim of an elder, he would ruin the peace and unity of the church (Ephesians 4:3).

11. *'not a lover of money'* (1 Timothy 3:3; compare Titus 1:7). Jesus made it plain that anyone who loves money cannot be a servant of God (Matthew 6:24). An elder who loves money can be bribed and bought off from speaking the truth of God as he should (Numbers 22:16-17). An elder is to be self-giving, not greedy for personal advantage. Love of money clogs the mind and produces worldliness in the conduct of church business. It leads to envy and strife.

12. *'managing his family well'* (1 Timothy 3:4-5; Titus 1:6). This is a man who leads his family firmly and yet with tenderness, in such a way that all the members of the family respect him and submit to him. There is a clear parallel between family responsibility and church responsibility, and the qualities required for the one are those needed also for the other.

The words of Paul in Titus 1:6 are not easy to interpret and so are difficult to apply in practice. 'A man whose children believe and are not open to the charge of being wild and disobedient.' Some people take them to mean that an elder's children must have saving faith, and we must respect that view. I think we must ask how long do we have to wait for saving faith to be given? Taken to its logical conclusion, no man with children can safely be appointed an elder until his children come to saving faith or until they die! Also this seems to make parents responsible for the saving faith of their children, ignoring that it is a gift of God. Again a father can only

have responsibility for his children while they are in his house, so
that the test can only apply to children at home. In that context it
would be very difficult for a man to be an elder while his children
were openly denying the faith either by their words or by their
actions. A distinction has to be made between unruliness and the
immaturity and exuberance of youth. But we have to recognise that
some children are naturally rebellious and difficult to handle despite
belonging to the most godly family. The question then becomes, to
what extent the parents have sought to teach and train their children.
The end product can often be better than they deserve; it can also be
much worse. This is the kind of mature evaluation that must be made
when a man is suitable in every other respect.

The Bible commentator Dr.John Gill wrote:

> By faithful children (AV) cannot be meant converted ones
> or true believers in Christ; for it is not in the power of men to
> make their children such; and their not being so can never be
> an objection to their being elders, if otherwise qualified; at the
> most the phrase can only intend that they should be brought
> up in the faith, in the principles, doctrines and ways of
> Christianity.

13. *'not a recent convert'* (1 Timothy 3:6). This is a gracious provision in the interests of both the man and the church (1 Timothy 5:22).
A good man will not spoil for being given a little time to mature
before taking up the work.

14. *'good reputation'* (1 Timothy 3:7). This is the positive side of the
first requirement to be 'above reproach'. Neighbours and work-
mates may not like a man's religion but they will admit his integrity.

15. *'not overbearing'* (Titus 1:7). The word 'overbearing' is the
opposite to 'gentle' because it reflects a fixed attitude of mind or
inflexibility. It involves arrogance and lack of consideration for the
position, feelings or opinions of others. The cure for this is for elders
to remember they are fallen people saved by grace, dealing with
fallen people saved by grace. If this does not give them gentleness,
humility and patience, nothing will.

16. *'not quick tempered'* (Titus 1:7) is akin to 'not violent' (9 above).

17. *'a lover of good'* (Titus 1:8). This includes both spiritual things
and the good things in life generally as Paul indicates in Philippians
4:8.

18. *'upright'* (Titus 1:8). Implies honesty and fair dealing, trustworthiness and faithfulness in every relationship.

19. *'holy'* (Titus 1:8) This is a life of purity, the fruit of living as in the presence of God (Genesis 17:1; Ephesians 1:4). In 1 Peter 5:3 the apostle tells elders they are to be examples to the flock. This surely means they are to show the way in faith, hope and love (1 Corinthians 13:13) and in humility and holiness.

You might think that elders can never be found because no man can possibly meet all these requirements. We must not play down the force of these characteristics; they are set before us by the Lord. But it seems to me that a man may be appointed if he does not obviously, glaringly, violate any of these requirements, in such a way as to hinder the exercise of his ministry as an elder, and if he displays growth in the areas where he is weakest.

The qualifications of elders

It can be argued that 1 Timothy 3 and Titus 1 do little more than give us a comprehensive view of the godly life to which all believers are called. We might add that elders should be outstanding examples of such a life and that would be right. But it seems to me that in these two passages Paul was not giving a complete 'job specification' of elders. This becomes obvious when we realise that a person may be well above the average in the characteristics Paul describes and yet still be a hopeless elder. What then is true of an elder that may not be true of other members in the church?

The qualifications we are looking for are not easy to define, but I think they must be in the area of gifts. This can be gleaned from a consideration of what I have said in chapters six to eleven, and chapters twenty to twenty-four. In some cases the significant factor will be Holy Spirit empowered preaching. In others it will be the gift of leadership. Then there are outstanding gifts of personal counselling, group teaching, personal evangelism and the training of others. Some have an ability to weld other people into a team, some inspire love, zeal for the health of the church, or enthusiasm for the gospel. Very often an appointment will be made because the particular gift possessed is the very one the church requires at a given time.

All elders must measure up to the requirements of 1 Timothy 3 and Titus 1. In addition to these an elder must be gifted in some way that benefits the church. At the risk of 'vain repetition' let me underline that no person should be expected to have all these gifts. One elder may be exceptionally gifted, but it is not a qualification that any should possess all of them. One suitable gift is enough, no more and no less should be expected of any elder but if the Lord equips someone with more than one gift, it is a bonus for which the church should be thankful.

Questions

1 What does Titus 1:6 mean? In what circumstances should it be used as a reason to ask an elder to stand down?
2 What defects in an elder would negate his ministry to you?

Appendix

I am indebted to my friends Richard Chester and John Appleby, elders of the church at Abingdon, for the use of the following 'Proposal for Eldership'. They have prepared this form to help members of a church carefully work through the biblical requirements of an elder, before making any proposal. It is suggested that such proposal forms could be available on request for any member to use when it is felt that there is a need for appointing an elder to their fellowship.

PROPOSAL FOR ELDERSHIP

The proposal of an elder should be undertaken prayerfully and in the fear of the Lord. This sheet is prepared to help you, as a church member, face the biblical requirements of a man for such a ministry. Read the scriptures referred to and answer 'yes' or 'unsure', to all questions. Try to make an honest assessment but remember that only God is perfect.

1. **His experience.** Elder means 'older man' (see the use of the word in

1 Timothy 5:1). 'Older' is a relative term and will depend to some extent on the age of others in the church and eldership. To serve as an elder, a younger man should have a mental and spiritual maturity well beyond his years. He should not be a recent convert (1 Timothy 3:6).

Is he of an age and experience to lead in this particular church?   ✔ as necessary

Yes	Unsure

2. **His character.**   1 Timothy 3:1-7; Titus 1:6-9. The qualifications listed are not exhaustive and arise from the particular circumstances of the first century. Most of the items reflect outward, observable behaviour. Certain things are taken for granted and covered by other scriptures but these passages give an indication of requirements in some general areas.

a. Is he above reproach in his marriage, family and home life?

b. Is he self-controlled — in temper, appetites and finances?

c. Is he gentle in spirit — not quarrelsome?

d. Has he a good reputation with outsiders?

3. **His godliness.** Galatians 5:22,23.

Is the fruit of the Spirit evident in his life?

4. **His ability.** Elders are responsible before God to the Shepherd of the flock. Acts 20:28; 1 Peter 5:2.

a. Could he direct the affairs of the church? 1 Timothy 5:17.

b. Can he admonish, teach and encourage others in the truth? 1 Thessalonians 5:12; 1 Timothy 3:2; Titus 1:9
.

c. Can he refute error? Acts 20:30-32; Titus 1:9.

d. Is he an example to the flock? Hebrews 13:7; 1 Peter 5:3.

5. **His attitude.**

a. Is he willing and eager to serve? 1 Peter 5:2.

b. Has he a 'servant spirit? Mark 10:42-45; 1 Peter 5:3.

c. Can he work well with others? Philippians 2:3-5.

Having thoughtfully and prayerfully considered the matter I would like to propose .... as an elder of the church.

Signature .... Date ....

Please do not mention your proposal to anyone except the present elders to whom this entire form should be given. Your name as proposer will not be made public.

Further comments (if necessary)

14.
Appointing elders — church preparation

Elders arrive in the first place by a number of different routes. Missionaries may oversee a church they have founded and take it on to the appointment of leaders. Some churches grow spontaneously and their leaders may be obvious from the beginning. Others may need the help of trusted elders from nearby churches to provide the ministry required or to show them the way to make suitable appointments. Some will have an existing eldership and others will move from a one pastor situation to plurality. Whatever the setting the process of making appointments should be preceded by spiritual preparation.

Writing under the title 'Perturbed', Wilfred Kuhrt has said,

> No one who has kept his ear to the ground can have failed to notice the large number of churches and pastors that have been in trouble of late... How do we go about the appointment of pastors, elders, deacons? Is there sufficient prayer and waiting upon the Lord, perhaps with fasting (Acts 13:2-3)? For how long a period before decisions are made? Is there adequate vetting of the man and his family...?
>
> *(Grace* Magazine)

And Mr. Kuhrt is not alone in his concern.

The ideal is for a church always to be spiritually healthy but there are certain times when this is of paramount importance. One of those times is the appointment of elders. The example of our Lord spending all night in prayer before appointing the twelve (Luke

6:12-16) and of the church at Antioch 'fasting and praying' before setting apart two evangelists (Acts 13:1-3) should be enough to prove the necessity of spiritual preparation before elders are appointed. This is so important that we will underline it with two reasons:

The first reason is that we are not dealing with a piece of human organisation; the church is not a social club, a political party nor a business concern. A church should be a very friendly place — but it is still not a social club; there should be efficient organisation, but the church is not a business concern. It is a spiritual body — a group of people redeemed by the precious blood of Jesus Christ, united to him by the Holy Spirit and energised, controlled and directed by the same Holy Spirit, according to the Scriptures. The Head of the church, the Lord Jesus Christ, instructs all his members by his Holy Spirit through the Word. This means that the guiding factor in the appointing of elders is not human wisdom but the will of Christ as it is revealed to us. The existence of a party spirit or of personal animosities is contrary to a spiritual atmosphere. Divisions of this kind not only achieve nothing positive, they actually destroy the church.

When Paul wrote to the Corinthian church he had to say: 'Brothers, I could not address you as spiritual but as worldly—mere infants in Christ...You are still worldly. For since there is jealousy and quarrelling among you, are you not worldly? Are you not acting like mere men? For when one says, "I follow Paul", and another "I follow Apollos" are you not mere men?' (1 Corinthians 3: 1-3). In verse 16 of the same chapter Paul says, 'Don't you know that you yourselves are God's temple and that God's Spirit lives in you? If anyone destroys God's temple, God will destroy him.' In these matters we stand before a holy God. Spiritual health is absolutely vital because we are dealing with a spiritual body not a mere organisation.

The second reason for the necessity of spiritual health is that the process of appointing elders has to be spiritual and not mechanical. The actual process through which the church goes must be seen to be, and felt to be, a spiritual exercise. There are no biblical rules to guide us in the actual process — every situation is different, so a great deal depends on the spirituality of the men involved and on the spirituality of the church. The reason why this process has to be a spiritual one is that the task required of elders is a spiritual one. The ministry of elders has to do with the ministry of God's Word. The primary thing with which these men are concerned is to protect the church, and to instruct the members concerning God's truth. They are to care for the souls of people as those who must give an account to God for that ministry (Hebrews 13:17). For example, if people are going astray there has to be a spiritual ministry — it is not just laying down the law or having a set of rules all must keep; that is mere organisation. A spiritual ministry is a delicate, tender matter applying the Holy Spirit's instruction in the Word, dealing gently with the souls of men and women and young people that are being prepared for everlasting glory.

Elders must be able constantly to discern the guiding hand of God; they have a body of people under their spiritual care and questions will arise. Elders are not merely to say 'this is a very good thing to do' or 'this is commonsense, everybody knows this is the right thing to do', but must be sensitive to the Lord's leading through his Word. The great aim is to present everyone perfect in Christ (Colossians 1:28). Therefore as their task is a spiritual one the appointment of elders requires a spiritual process. Before any one of us says, 'I think this person will make a good elder, I'm sure of it' we must examine ourselves to see if we are in a fit state spiritually to have a discerning eye on the matter.

The process of appointing elders involves the delicate responsibility of assessing men, determining whether they have certain qualifications, attributes or gifts; so the church must exercise spiritual discernment. There must be spiritual honesty that rids us of prejudice and of emotive arguments, and really faces situations in the light of the Word of God.

Sometimes people say, 'I like Mr. So and So, he's a nice man.' That's good but it doesn't mean he has the qualities of an elder. Someone else will say, 'He's very loving, very easy going.' So be it! But that is neither spiritual discernment nor spiritual honesty. Honesty requires that we ask ourselves why we favour this man. Is it simply because we like him or get on well with him? We should get on well with all the men in the church! But that doesn't mean any of them have the quality of elders. We may say, 'This man has great Bible knowledge,' but even that does not necessarily qualify him to be an elder. He may have all the Bible knowledge in the world and be the most impossible man to work with. Again we may say, 'This man is holy,' but surely all members of the church should be holy.

Does the mere fact that a man is likeable, nice, loving, easy to get on with, knowledgeable and holy, qualify him to be an elder? Not necessarily, because all of us ought to be all those things, and yet not all of us are meant to be elders. So we must come to the Word of God with honesty, with spiritual discernment and spiritual understanding of what is required.

The whole church must give itself to prayer and self-examination (Acts 14:23). In my experience, discussion in a church about eldership leads sooner or later to spiritual self-scrutiny. The church asks, 'Where do we fall short in the gifts that are needed for a fuller life of the church?' We should encourage the church to pray for those gifts, to examine its own life until those gifts are discerned and then to appoint the men with those gifts.

Along with these things must be adequate instruction in the church about the qualifications of elders, and all that needs to be taken into account before elders are appointed. This should not be hurried, but time given for discussion about the principles involved before ever names are mentioned.

Before elders are appointed, a number of practical issues need to be discussed and agreement reached about them. The most important of these we have already dealt with in chapters seven to fourteen. There also needs to be agreement about the process to be followed in making these appointments.

Questions

1 What qualities make a person suitable for leadership apart from the spiritual qualifications set out in 1 Timothy 3:2-13?
2 How can you discover hidden gifts and talents among the members of your church?

15.
Appointing elders — a process

Two opposite procedures have been adopted. The first has been the appointment of elders by existing leaders with little, or in some cases no reference to the church members. Warrant for this has been found mainly in two texts, Acts 14:23 and Titus 1:5.

In Acts 14:23 elders were 'appointed' by Paul and Barnabas. I have already argued that we do not have people with apostolic authority in the churches today, and that we may not take our example from the actions of the apostles. In addition to that, the word used for 'appointed' here seems to imply the 'stretching out of the hands'. At the risk of being accused of arguing from silence, I would suggest that since the apostle Paul expected a church to act as a whole in matters of discipline, (e. g. 1 Corinthians 5:4-5) it is unlikely that the church members in Acts 14:23 were not consulted or involved in any way in appointing elders. But, even if the idea is rejected in this case, there was good reason for the exercise of apostolic authority in these early days of church founding. We are a long way on from there.

I believe we must deal with Titus 1:5 in the same way, though a different word is used. William Hendriksen comments 'Though Paul says, "that you may appoint" (AV) he by no means excludes the responsible co-operation of the individual congregation (see Acts 1:15-26; 6:1-6; note the same verb in Acts 6:2)'. (*New Testament Commentary, Timothy and Titus,* page 345).

We may also take into consideration the fact that those appointed as elders are to lead the church, which means the church is expected to follow them. This being so, it is reasonable that the members are given some part in the process of appointment. People are much more likely to respect one in whose appointment they have had some part than one foisted upon them with little or no consultation. There is little point in the shepherd being out in the front if the sheep are a long way behind.

The other extreme is leaving the whole matter to a process of nomination by the members and accepting a majority vote by the church often with inadequate instruction, and a minimum of supervision on the part of the leaders. This is the highroad to chaos and in the past has been one of the prime causes of churches losing their theological moorings.

There are no clear instructions laid down in Scripture for the exact procedure to be used in appointing elders. This leaves room for considerable flexibility taking into account the differing conditions and situation of each church. I believe the suggestions I am making here harmonise with Scripture principles, but I have been influenced also by my own experience and the experience of others.

In harmony with the principles we have already discussed, the first part of the process is to assess the gifts, qualities and talents the Lord has given to members of the church. The aim of any church must be to ensure that so far as possible every gift is used to the full, and that leadership arises from within the church. This applies as much to elders set apart for teaching and preaching as to the other elders. A church should not automatically look outside its own membership for a full-time preaching elder.

The next step is to assess what biblical ministries are not being fulfilled. If there are men qualified to be elders, then they should be appointed. If such men are not available then the church must give itself to prayer for the Lord to give men suitably qualified. Such men may move into the church or the church may have to wait prayerfully and patiently for them to arise from within the membership. Or, as has traditionally happened men may be called from other churches to meet the need. No amount of pressure should be allowed to lead to the appointment of unsuitable people. Biblical requirements and a sense of need should lead to prayer first, not to precipitous action.

The desirability of new appointments may be brought to the church by the elders. This could arise from the elders themselves or it could be prompted by comments from the members. Either elders or members may feel there is a need, or that there are suitable men in the church who should be appointed. For example, perhaps a certain man over a period of time has exhibited a high degree of spirituality in prayer and godliness; he has made significant advance in the development and use of suitable gifts, and in an ability to lead and encourage others.

Need can be measured by the size of the membership (say two elders for a membership up to twenty; three up to a membership of fifty; four up to a membership of a hundred; five up to a hundred and fifty). But some churches are beset by more problems than others often depending on the area in which the church is set, therefore it is better to be guided by gifts available and ministries needed than by the provisions of a constitution. It may be the Lord has given more gifts to members than the church has needed hitherto. This is a responsibility to be taken seriously. Questions should be asked. Is the Lord pointing to work being neglected in the church? Is the Lord wanting us to help other churches? Gifts should not be allowed to run to seed.

The eldership ought always to consider how the gifts given to individuals can be used in the fullest and best possible way, not only for the interests of the local church, but for the wider church as well. At times this may require that the most talented pastors move out to the mission field. If a pastor shows increasing ability in evangelism and is frequently called on by other churches, it may be necessary for him to consider a full-time itinerant ministry and for the elders to consider it with him.

> (Erroll Hulse, *Shepherding God's flock*
> Sprinkle Publications)

The members can be asked to suggest names in writing to the existing elder or elders. Some would argue that the nominee should give his permission before his name is suggested, and I respect that view. My own preference however, would be that such permission is not sought in advance of consideration by the elders. This avoids embarrassment if the nomination is deemed unsuitable by the elders. In such a case the elders are obliged to explain their reasons to the members who made the nomination but the person nominated is not troubled. This is where the interplay of trust, love and mutual submission is so important. The reasons for the unsuitability of a man to be appointed an elder may need to be dealt with; but this should be done pastorally and not in the context of a nomination. A further argument for not approaching the person first is that he may refuse permission for his name to be nominated for any number of reasons including sheer humility. But that same person confronted with the overwhelming wishes of the whole church is compelled to think seriously before rejecting his nomination.

And then in the light of the nominations, and of their own independent thoughts the elders bring the names that they now recommend before the church. Time is given, perhaps one or two months for prayer, and for any questions to be asked privately of the elders. At this time those nominated and considered suitable by the elders would be made aware of the fact and any practical problems ironed out. For example, a man's business commitments may be such that he would not be able to give the necessary time to this ministry unless he was willing and able to make changes. Health and family considerations may also be involved. A man may be entirely suitable and yet not be appointed if he is for some practical reason unable to fulfil this ministry.

Where there are no practical impediments the man being considered must be given time to wait on the Lord. He may have been prepared by the Lord but still needs humbly to look for his confirmation. The 'peace of Christ' must rule in his heart (Colossians 3:15). If the matter is taken further by the church, the man must seek the Lord's cleansing from wrong thoughts, motives and desires, and his enabling for the task that lies ahead.

Next, a church meeting is held in the absence of those nominated, open to loving, frank, Bible-based discussion. If the way is not clear then the elders must take the matter back for re-consideration. The aim is whole church consensus and it is worth taking time to secure this.

At some point it is helpful for the church to be at liberty to question the proposed elders, after which the appointments are agreed at a final meeting in an atmosphere of love, thanksgiving and prayer.

A public 'setting apart' is desirable when hands may be laid on those appointed, thus committing them to the Lord's grace for the ministry to which they have now been appointed.

Questions

1 What evidence should you look for that the Lord is directing the
church to a certain person to invite as an elder?
a) from within the church?
b) from another church?

2 How can a church discover all it needs to know about a person
from another church without overstepping the bounds of delicacy
and decency?

16
Appointing elders — special cases

We must now consider two specific situations. The principles we have already discussed will generally still apply, but in these cases additional guidance may be helpful.

Where a plural eldership does not already exist

Where a plural eldership does not already exist and the church is led by a pastor with a group of deacons, the process of change can be hazardous. There are two issues that must be clearly understood during the teaching stage. These are, the nature of leadership in the church and the question of the parity of elders. If these questions are not settled then confusion will arise in the future decision making of the church.

The process for making the change must be thought through very carefully. For example, if the pastor acts on his own, making his own nominations and evaluating suggestions from the membership he may discover this is a very delicate matter. In the past such a procedure has sometimes resulted in serious misunderstanding, division and even resignations. It is best to approach the matter gradually. One way is to ensure that, from a certain point in time, all appointments to the diaconate are recognized as being either with 'elder' responsibility or with 'deacon' responsibility. All then work together until it seems right for a separation into a diaconate and an eldership to take place.

There are some advantages in this process. It means that the moment of separation has been anticipated and that there are men already recognized by the church for the eldership. When the time comes for proposals to be made to the church for a separate eldership, the church will have expressed its confidence in suitable people. It will then normally rest with the elders to make the final proposals. Also, if a pastorless period occurs before a separate eldership is established, there is a positive pastoral continuation.

Another way is possible if there is one brother in the membership in addition to the pastor who would be an obvious choice by all concerned, without question. Let that man be appointed and he will share the responsibility of further recommendations with the pastor. From a practical viewpoint it is often less than satisfactory to have only one other elder in addition to a man who is 'full-time'. The pastor plus two is more likely to be effective. But, if suitable men are not in the membership appointments should not be rushed, no matter what arguments may be used to the contrary. We mustn't establish an eldership 'at all costs' or simply 'to be in fashion'.

Then the attitude of the existing deacons is also important. They may feel they are being down-graded! Also, if one or more of their number are proposed for elders, the feelings of the others have to be gently ministered to. It may be best for all concerned to be asked to resign and a new start made; they all may be willing to accept what is recommended, but there is often a difference between how men honestly think they will react and what they actually do at the time of decision. We need to be very careful here. Everybody believes them when they say, 'Yes, we will accept whatever is suggested; yes, we are humble before God; yes we will accept it.' But, when the moment comes and one has not been nominated as an elder, despite how he honestly believed he would react, it just does not happen that way. The Devil knows well how to exploit such situations. Every care must be taken to ensure jealously or resentment do not arise. If they do, it should not affect the recommendations made; normally it will indicate the rightness of those recommendations. However, there must be sympathetic pastoral care of those who feel aggrieved. The full use of the gifts of those concerned should heal wounds in time. If not, then the normal biblical disciplines have to be applied.

When once a plural eldership has been established the church becomes aware of changes. We should be prepared for a period of transition. The teaching beforehand may have been most biblical and thoroughly practical but experience tells us that until members see the arrangement functioning many do not grasp what has been taught. A despairing pastor may wonder if he had ever taught them — or had he just been dreaming! Patience is needed and a willingness not to insist on ideals, at least in the beginning. Elders and deacons themselves take time to adjust in their new roles and the church must be patient with them.

Calling an elder from outside the church

Another situation is the calling of someone from outside the membership to be an elder. I hope we have put behind us the practice of earlier days where one church called a pastor from another church, with no reference to the latter. At the same time, the pastor gave no clue to his own deacons, much less the church, that he was moving until the whole matter was signed, settled and sealed.

When a church feels it has to look outside its own membership an attempt should be made to avoid taking an elder from the same position in another church. Again, there should be flexibility. Some men are more like evangelists, building up a church then moving to another. There are a variety of reasons why others may feel it right to make a change; but great care needs to be taken not to risk unsettling a good work without much prayer and very careful thought and investigation.

It is my opinion that no name should be 'floated' in an open church meeting before due consideration has been given to that person by the elders. Members should be encouraged to make the elders aware of their being drawn to a certain man. Elders will 'keep their ears to the ground' for indications of such drawing within the church. In some situations they may need to make a recommendation to the church apart from any moves by members, but gradually the Lord's guidance is seen in a general attraction for the right reasons to a particular man.

There is no substitute for trust between members and leaders. This trust is sometimes undermined if elders do not explain to the people why they think a man on whom the members seem keen does not have their support. Any positive recommendation should be presented to the church by the elders, and I believe it wise for the church to be required to consider only one name at a time.

When a church is without adequate leadership it is a good thing for them to ask a respected brother from another church to lead them until this lack is remedied. Such a brother is often called a moderator, but I can think of no reason why he should be given that or any other title.

If a church is calling a man from another fellowship, no matter what ministry he exercised there, that fellowship should be consulted from the beginning. There should be loving consultation between all concerned, seeking the mind of the Lord on the proposed move.

Perhaps the enquiries began after two or three preaching appointments during which the church felt unusual spiritual blessing. After careful enquiry from those who know the man best it may be that, after all, his gifts are not those required. There may be faults and limitations in the man, his wife or his family, not immediately apparent. I cannot emphasize too strongly the folly of looking for 'the archangel Gabriel'. Some churches seem unable to accept that they will never find the perfect man. The question is, are the imperfections in clear violation of the biblical qualifications? Are the faults such as to intrude into the minds of members while the man is exercising his pastoral ministry?

The process of investigation is a very delicate one; it must be thorough. The evidence of three or four of a man's best sermons is totally insufficient. Many a time onlookers have had to say, 'We knew it wouldn't work, why didn't they take the most elementary precautions?' This applies not only to the church's assessment of the man, but also to the man's assessment of the church. In the same way that the church may accept weaknesses in the man, so a man may be aware of great problems in a church. For example, the church may be divided or in danger of drifting theologically, but these things do not of necessity mean the man will refuse the invitation. The great thing is that he is not taken by surprise. He cannot know all about the church as would an elder appointed from within the membership; but he should know enough not to regret his move within a year of accepting the invitation.

While thorough research needs to be done by the church and the man, care must be taken not to indulge in 'witch hunting' or 'character assassination'. In these days people are accustomed to judging one another by their own standards caring little about the effects of their judgements on their victims. The good reputation of the church, and of the man and his wife must be preserved in an atmosphere of prayer and loving fellowship.

If a man from another church is under serious consideration he should be told about this when he is invited to make a return visit. He should be kept informed of the progress of discussions and especially he should know the precise significance of requests to preach. Is the request part of very early considerations or is it 'with a view' to an invitation to move to the church? If possible a man under consideration should be heard preaching in his present setting when he is unlikely to preach one of his best sermons, and when his relationship with church members can be observed.

After prayer and consultation the church may decide that a certain man does not suit their needs. If the man has been aware that he was being considered he should be told that he will not be invited and some reasons given for this decision.

If the matter is proceeding positively then leaders of both churches should meet. Also further opportunity should be given for the inviting church to meet the man, his wife and family, in informal gatherings, in the houses of members, as well as in a variety of more formal occasions.

From this point, procedures in the church can follow a pattern similar to the one we have already suggested for the appointment of elders.

Questions

1 If a man is bitter about not being appointed an elder, how will you minister to him?
2 How can a church get to know a man and his family before an invitation is given to him to become an elder?

17.
Relationship of elders with elders

In a family, growth is stimulated by the interplay of relationships. There is organisation (or should be!) — there is regulation (or should be!) — there is education (or should be!) — but a family can have organisation, regulation and education and be as cold as the freezer in the kitchen! The life of a family is in smooth running, loving, productive relationships of parent with parent, parents with children, and children with children — and of all with relatives, visitors, and neighbours. Those relationships can also be likened to the working of a body as Paul says in Ephesians 4:16: 'The whole body, joined and held together by every supporting ligament grows and builds itself up in love, as each part does its work.'

As in a family or a body, the life of a church is in its relationships — the whole church with the Lord, elders with elders, elders with deacons, elders and deacons with their wives, elders and deacons with the church, members with the leaders, and members with members.

We discussed the vital connection between Christ and the church in chapter four. After this nothing is more important than the relationship between elders and elders. I realise that for one reason or another some men having neither fellow elders or deacons with whom they can have fellowship at leadership level are alone. We must pray for such men that the Lord will give the help that they need.

Also many churches are led by one elder and a group of deacons where the deacons are exercising some degree of eldership responsibility. What we say about the relationship of elders with elders will very largely apply to them also.

It is vital that there should be effective fellowship among the elders. This is for the benefit of the elders themselves. At a time when without the fortifying of a group of fellow elders many pastors were suffering breakdowns in one form or another, the question was asked, 'Who pastors the pastor?' Plural eldership is not the whole answer to this question, indeed it is no answer at all if there is no effective fellowship between them, but if there is then this problem is greatly reduced. This fellowship is also vital for the church's sake. The members need to see in the eldership a picture of what the whole church should be like. The shepherding of the church begins with the example the elders give. Without this example there will be confusion and leadership will be unconvincing, failing to set the right tone for the life of the church as a whole. With this example other groups in the church such as deacons and youth leaders will see how they too should relate to each other. A breakdown of fellowship among the elders is like a malfunctioning heart valve.

The quality of the fellowship in a church rarely rises above the example given by the relationship between the leaders (Hosea 4:9; 2 Chronicles 12:6). Frequently the apostles were able to appeal to their own conduct as an example to the churches (1 Thessalonians 2:10).

What are the characteristics of this fellowship among elders? The *first and most important thing is love.* This is underlined by the amount of time and patience our Lord spent teaching the disciples to love each other, and forgive each other (John 13:34-35; 15:12-13; Matthew 18:21-22). The ideal is for the eldership to be composed of men with a variety of temperaments, social backgrounds, political views, and experiences. This is rather like the twelve disciples and the need for constant renewing of love and mutual esteem with such an eldership will be as great as it was for them. This love should be expressed in the elders' ministry to one another with a view to strengthening, comforting, encouraging, warning and counselling. Such caring for each other will only be effective in the context of prayer and mutual submission to the Lord.

It is important that elders listen to one another and grow in an understanding of the strengths and weaknesses of each other, and in bearing patiently with each other's faults and shortcomings. The apostle Paul delighted to acknowledge how much his fellow workers meant to him. He took every opportunity to commend their strengths and to thank God for them (Romans 16: 3,9,21; Philippians 2:19-30).

There is also the need of *humbly recognising differing abilities* and of submitting to each other. This is especially needful as gifts of leadership emerge in certain areas. It may be natural for a full-time elder to take the lead in a general way. He is in the best position to know all that is happening in the church. But it is by no means true that a preaching elder is the best leader. Some preaching elders are the most hopeless organisers and the most inept at conducting meetings of elders or church meetings. Submission to each other in such ways must not lead to jealousy but to thankfulness that the Lord has given such gifts to his church.

This is the kind of relationship that must exist if right decisions are going to be made. Normally the aim will be to seek unanimity on matters to be commended to the church.

Elders must be careful not to give the impression that they exist to protect themselves or that their manner of life is never to be questioned. Leaders are always exposed to gossip and for the most part they should be like their Master who 'did not retaliate' (1 Peter 2:23). But when serious accusations are made against an elder, the rest must protect him from slander and injustice. Only when the evidence warrants, should the elders 'entertain an accusation against an elder' (1 Timothy 5:19-20) and take the appropriate action. In a case of immorality, persistent doctrinal error, or anything else that publicly dishonours the Lord, an elder must not be allowed to continue in his ministry.

A very delicate matter among elders is *watching over one another's spiritual state*. Theoretically a plural eldership should minimise the temptation to pride because no elder is above his brothers. However, elders can suffer from self-esteem as a group and this will destroy their ministry, and the love and trust the members may have for them. But an individual elder may succumb to pride, the most subtle of Satanic temptations. This can arise from a false view of one's own importance, wisdom or abilities. The tell-tale signs are the dominating of discussions, despising the gifts of others, and irritation when others disagree. Elders should live very near to the cross of Christ.

When men exalt themselves as something special in Christ's kingdom, the honour of their names and offices become equated with the cause of Christ. Eventually image-polishing becomes more important to them than the well-being of the sheep. A parent begins to care more deeply about the family reputation than the welfare of his children. A teacher's honour becomes of greater importance to him than assisting a troubled student. Defending the eldership becomes the chief priority of a church, for which the sheep may have to be sacrificed. We who are in positions of authority must carefully guard against this tendency in ourselves, and we must also be on the watch for it in those who are over us.

(Walter F. Chantry, *Shepherding God's flock* Sprinkle Publications)

Elders who are prosperous in business must beware of the pride which fails to realise that their comparative affluence can tempt others to jealousy. They should be willing to scale down their standard of living to reduce the possibility of this temptation, and as an example to others in this materialistic age.

There are special temptations that come to men who are taken from secular employment to full-time eldership. They may be tempted to carelessness because they are now responsible for how they use their time. Or, for the same reason they may overload themselves because they are not able to exercise control over their commitments. Fellow elders need to be aware of these problems and to be watchful for signs of either slackness or overloading.

A special watch needs to be given to preaching elders, in order that they may spend as much time as possible in reading and prayer. They need to be encouraged in this and not so loaded with other work that these things are squeezed out. Neglect here will adversely affect the spiritual health of the church.

Elders need also to be watchful over each other to maintain physical health and to cope with stress resulting from the pressures of life.

Elders' meetings should be characterised by prayer and openness. There is no need for formal minutes to be taken, but it is helpful if a note is made of specific decisions and of actions each person has been asked to take. Such a note can be available at the next meeting for the purposes of progress reports. Chairmanship of elders' meetings can helpfully be taken in rotation, but perhaps smooth working is more readily achieved by this being given to the most suitable person, who may not be a full-time elder. The principles upon which any part of the work of the church is undertaken should be thrashed out by the whole church. When these are agreed an individual elder may be asked to take responsibility for a particular ministry. He should be given scope to guide that work and develop it in his own way; any radical changes he proposes should be discussed first with the rest of the elders so that they all take the ultimate overall responsibility for all the work of the church. If there is praise or blame this is to be shared by all.

Elders should come to terms with the fact that it is not sinful for them to have differences in judgment in many matters; and elders should be willing to share with the church difficult matters which are not confidential. They should not hesitate in some difficult cases to seek the counsel of wise and experienced members of the church and not feel that in doing so their own dignity and authority is threatened. Paul goes even further than that and tells the Corinthians to 'appoint as judges even men of little account in the church' (1 Cor- inthians 6:4).

(Erroll Hulse, *Shepherding God's flock,*
Sprinkle Publications)

This would seem to me to be very wise advice where elders disagree among themselves.

A similar kind of procedure can also be happily applied to deacons' meetings.

People in the church other than elders may be gifted for preaching, evangelism or some other ministry and calls for the exercise of those gifts may come from other churches. Since the elders are responsible to the Lord for the spiritual welfare of all the members such people should submit to them for direction in the use of their gifts. The church should recognise these gifts and should send the members out with the church's recommendation and prayer support. None should go from the church without such recognition. It may be necessary for the elders to limit the appointments taken by a member for ministry elsewhere. Such considerations as family responsibilities, their own spiritual welfare, or the needs of their church may give rise to some restriction being applied. This will need to be decided in a prayerful and loving spirit. It is very desirable that these members should report back to the church occasionally, to stimulate prayer and to assess if their time and talents are being used to the best advantage for the Lord's glory.

The question arises as to the relationship of preachers and evangelists with the leaderships of their own church. To me it seems wrong when people travel hither and thither to help other churches when their own church is in desperate need of their gifts. Many churches in the past have sunk into a low condition while their own men have been 'filling pulpits' in other places every Sunday. Each situation will be different, but I believe normally men should only go to other churches if their own does not suffer as a result. A man may protest that God has called him to itinerant preaching, but I would need a lot of convincing that robbing one church to meet the need of another is wisdom from God.

It also seems odd to me that a man should receive a call for the eldership of another church when he has not been involved in that responsibility in his own fellowship.Such involvement should surely be the natural preparation for leadership elsewhere. But realistically a man's commitments may be such that he has not the time to go preaching elsewhere as well as being an active leader in his own church. Equally realistically, to include all preachers on the church's eldership may overload it. Perhaps the answer is to devise a scheme of training. Preachers could be invited to elders' meetings; they could also be asked to stop preaching for a period, during which time they could be used in practical ways in the church, thus learning from experience. At the same time they could discuss with other elders in depth the responsibilities of leadership.

Where there is but one elder with a number of deacons, problems arise when he accepts an invitation to another church. In the past this has been a common occurrence and often the bereft church has been ill-prepared for a 'pastorless period' and the challenge of seeking another leader. It may seem impertinent of me to question the assumption that such moves are prompted by the Lord's guidance, but I seriously suggest that sometimes they have a more human motivation. There may have been unwillingness or inability to face problems and the temptation to think the 'grass is greener' in another place. There may be an unrecognised personal ambition for an easier financial situation, or a sub-conscious career-mentality. Before we bridle at such a suggestion we should try to remember how seldom we have heard of a man going to a less promising situation.

However, the evidence may be overwhelming that the Lord is leading a man to move to another church. The question then arises as to how much teaching he has given to the church about the principles on which guidance has to be sought, about the things to be considered when inviting a new leader, and about the process of decision-making to be followed. No man should leave a church until he has done his best to prepare them for the change and if possible to help them find a new leader.

Questions

1 If elders fall out with each other what can be done about it?

2 If elders are unable to agree among themselves on a vital matter, what can they do?

18.
Elders' physical and mental well-being

Plural eldership is of little value if the elders do not watch over one another with loving care. In addition to caring for the spiritual health of each other they should also be sensitive to the physical and mental well-being of their colleagues, especially those full-time in the work.

Physical well-being

Every walk of life has its own problems and physical hazards and we should not wrap preaching elders up in cotton wool or give them any more attention than other members. But often preaching elders do not sufficiently care for themselves in their concern to minister to others. A common problem is a 'preacher's stomach' which affects what they eat before and after preaching, and demands the inclusion of 'Maclean's' or some other remedy in their brief case!

It may be necessary to remind colleagues that it is neither spiritual nor biblical to be careless about the needs of their bodies (1 Thessalonians 5:23; 1 Corinthians 6:19; 2 Timothy 2:20-21; 3 John 2).

Elders should be God-honouring in their attitude to food, exercise, relaxation and sleep. They should be an example to others in avoiding gluttony and drunkenness (1 Corinthians 10:31), avoiding obsession with diets and endless talk of calories. A rumbling stomach does not help a counselling session nor a prayer meeting so it is wise to determine the *diet* that is most suitable in order that preaching or counselling is unhindered. Nothing will undermine their physical well-being more seriously than failure to eat regularly and sensibly. In any case persistent and careless irregularity is sheer discourtesy to the cook!

All kinds of physical weaknesses arise from lack of *exercise*, and our mental alertness is often impaired for lack of a good breath of fresh air, or the exercise of our limbs. Discipline is obviously involved in avoiding over-indulgence but 'physical training is of some value' (1 Timothy 4:8).

Closely linked to exercise is *relaxation*, especially the easing of tension. We say it is 'all in the mind' but the effects are felt in the whole person.

We need to recognise that we function on a pattern of alternating contraction and relaxation, or to put it more simply of alternating work and rest. Our muscles contract and relax; our hearts contract and relax about seventy times a minute; our stomachs work after a meal and then need to rest awhile before we eat again; our minds are capable of hard work which must then be followed by rest. God, who made us, gave two laws to his people in the wilderness which are based on this law of our make-up; those two laws are 'Thou shalt work ... thou shalt rest' (Exodus 34:21). The principle behind those two laws has not altered, and yet numbers of Christians today are ignoring the second ...

It is not unspiritual to acknowledge that we are severely limited in what we can accomplish, and that we need our times of rest and relaxation. On the contrary it brings a childlike peace and simplicity to admit that we are indeed, 'frail children of dust and feeble as frail'. What a joy to know that 'he knows our frame, he remembers that we are dust'(Psalm 103:14).

(*A mind at ease,* Marion L Ashton, M.B. page 32,
Overcomer Literature Trust)

Sleep is also important. Too much sleep can mean too little time for prayer and meditation, and can lead to sluggishness of mind and body. However, I suspect the greater problem is to do with lack of sleep. If occasion demands we should be willing for this, but if we become tired and irritable we must examine our habits. We must not make rules for others but I would confess that over the years I have sometimes slept for half an hour after a mid-day meal, this enabled me at certain times to do an amount of work that surprised my friends. Let every person be persuaded in his own mind!

Coping with stress

The reasons for stress are varied, but there are commonly recognised causes. Elders, especially preaching elders, are always in the public eye and this in itself puts them under pressure. Their family also has the same problem and the elder has the responsibility of caring for his family as well as coping with himself. Then there is the effect of knowing the high expectations people have of their elders both in their conduct and in their ministry. This is especially the case if members have in their minds the example of an outstanding man known to them. A sense of high calling and commitment leads elders to a very full-time occupation. A plural eldership should minimise this pressure so that one man does not feel he must be available twenty-four hours a day, seven days a week. But conscience is a hard taskmaster and elders sometimes allow themselves to feel that an evening at home or a day out with the family is a dereliction of duty.

A full-time elder and his wife, even when surrounded by other elders and deacons, can feel lonely. This is because their fellow leaders have freedom to withdraw from responsibilities when extra burdens come on them, but the full-time family must stay with the work through thick and thin. They are human — they have feelings and their feelings can be badly hurt.

Paul Beasley-Murray in *Pastors under pressure* (Kingsway Publications) mentions causes of pressure such as financial worries, few quantifiable results, the success of others, the complexity of moral issues and the higher educational standards in our congregations. Dr. Beasley Murray says:

> Stress in itself is not to be feared. As far as ministers are concerned it is excess stress (hyper stress) which is to be feared. The term currently being used to describe the negative effect of too much stress is 'strain'. It is strain which causes heart disease. Or to put it in other terms: tension in itself will

not kill us. It is continual tension without relief which becomes dangerous.

I usually feel the effects of stress at times when I am not under
pressure. It is especially noticed during the first few days of a
holiday when I am given to much yawning! This has taught me to
beware of allowing pressure to build up without control even when
I feel fit and able to cope. Some time ago when I had not learnt this
lesson I was suffering from strain that put me out of action. The Lord
graciously drew my attention to the fact that in Jesus Christ he is my
heavenly Father. He showed me that I was living at a constant
tension as though his work depended entirely on me. He taught me
to rely on him instead of myself and to 'rest' in the midst of my
wrestling. The outcome was ability to do far more work than ever
before but to do so in a more relaxed way.

An advantage of plural eldership is the means it provides for
elders to watch over one another and to prevent stress occuring, if
possible, and where it does occur to see the signs and minister to the
brother concerned. There are often practical measures to take, such
as relieving the brother from some, if not all, of his duties for a time.
Spiritual ministry is called for, seeking to counsel the brother about
his relationship to the Lord.

There are signs of stress that can be fairly easily observed. A
normally cheerful person becomes morose; a usually quiet person
becomes excitable. Or there is an irrational swing from one state to
another, an inconsistency of emotion that makes it impossible for
others to know what to expect. A sudden display of temper, dis-
satisfaction, or some other reaction totally out of character may also
be a tell-tale warning that all is not well.

This is not the place to spell out the problem and answers to it in
greater detail. Since elders are called to minister to members of their
congregation who are under stress they should be able to help one
another. But there are two opposite dangers to avoid. One is to treat
the aberration of an elder too lightly; for example, an elder loses his
temper in a church meeting. Whatever the reasons, action should be
taken to indicate that the other elders take a serious view of it. If the
lapse happens frequently then it may be necessary to relieve the
brother of his ministry temporarily or permanently. But the opposite danger is to deal with such a man too harshly. No one should
expect perfection of any elder, and allowance should be made for

the circumstances surrounding the lapse. The man should be embraced in love and understanding, and on an expression of repentance before the church, he should be accepted with assurances of prayer and mutual confidence.

Questions

1 What would you say to a Christian worker who believed it right for him or her to 'burn out for the Lord'?
2 Assess your own physical, mental and psychological stamina.

19.
Relationship of elders with deacons

The second relationship we must explore in the church is that between elders and deacons. Before we discuss the practical problems to be resolved we need to emphasise attitudes of mind in both elders and deacons. All are no more and no less than members of the church. They are not on the outside looking in; they are not above the church looking down on it; rather they are ministering to the church from within, equally submissive to the Word and to one another. Furthermore, all are no more and no less than servants of the church. All leadership in the local church is 'deaconing' (ministering — serving, Acts 6: 1-2; Matthew 20:24-28) and this with a view to the whole church being a caring, serving community. 'There are deacons within the community of deacons' (*Toward a fresh look at the diaconate*, I. M. Stringer).

Deacons are to be no less spiritually minded than elders. A study of 1 Timothy 3:2-13 will show that many of the qualities required of elders are also required of deacons. But deacons must also be 'sincere' which is literally 'not double tongued'(AV). They must 'keep hold of the deep truths of the faith with a clear conscience'. As with elders they must be subject to testing before they are appointed. The men chosen to 'wait on tables' in Acts 6:1-6 were 'full of the Spirit and wisdom', and of one of them, Stephen, it is said he was 'full of faith and of the Holy Spirit'. These men were not specifically labelled deacons but there is good reason to see them as a diaconate in embryo. This same passage gives us clues about the appointment of deacons. The work was recommended by the apostles because of an existing need, so we see that the duties of deacons need not be specified in advance, but they can be appointed to deal with a present situation or as needs arise.

The church chose the men who were then approved by the apostles. This suggests a procedure similar to that adopted for the appointment of elders, namely inter-action between members and leaders, with the leaders having the final word.

There is also a hint here as to the relationship between elders and deacons. Deacons were appointed to relieve the apostles of work that would take them away from their primary duties of praying and preaching. The basic principle is that deacons are appointed by the church to serve the church, mainly in assisting the elders so that the latter can do their work unhindered by day to day administration. Elders and deacons are not separate entities nor does their work merely overlap, but that of the deacons is a sub-section of the work which falls upon elders, namely, to lead the church; the work of deacons is delegated to them by the elders. John Benton, in another church Bible study paper, has gathered the following biblical evidence:

1   The elders of the church are responsible before God for the whole flock in every single department (Acts 20:28). There is no area of which the elders can ultimately say 'that is not our responsibility, it is solely a matter for the deacons'. This is explicit in 1 Timothy 5:17 where without reference to deacons and without qualification, Paul speaks of the elders as 'directing the affairs of the church'.

2   That general principle seems to be acted upon in the New Testament history. When churches are planted on Paul's first missionary tour, having given them time to settle and for people's gifts to emerge, the apostle goes back with Barnabas, and appoints, not elders and deacons, but just elders (Acts 14:23). Titus, in charge of the growing work in Crete, is told to ordain elders (Titus 1:5). Again there is no mention of deacons.

Were the deacons already there in both cases? That would be an assumption from silence. No, it seems that, to begin with, elders alone are charged with responsibility for the church. This is in notable contrast to the order in which elders and deacons usually emerge in modern churches.

3   On a number of occasions elders are spoken of as doing what many would term 'deacons' work'. After the prophecy of Agabus, a collection is made in Antioch for the church in Jerusalem. It is sent by the hands of Paul and Barnabas, not to the deacons (or 'proto-deacons' of Acts 6), but to the elders of Jerusalem (Acts 11:30). Finance may have been delegated to the deacons but if so, this did not mean that the elders took no part in it whatsoever.

Again in Acts 20, Paul is addressing the Ephesian elders. He warns and encourages them to guard themselves and the flock. But at the end of what he had to say (vv.32-35) he charges them with overall responsibility for caring for the weak and the poor. The elders do not turn round and say, 'Paul, why are you telling us this, it is deacons' work?' They accepted overall responsibility. Furthermore the care of the sick is expressly assigned to the elders in James 5:14.

4   In Acts 6:1-6 the question arises as to why the apostles did not take on the job of 'serving tables'. Was it because they were not gifted for it? Was it because it was not their responsibility? Was it because the work was beneath them? Certainly not! It was simply a matter of priorities for time and effort. They must give themselves to prayer and the ministry of the word in order to help this large Jerusalem flock. The job in Jerusalem was *delegated* which implies the apostles recognised it as their responsibility ultimately. The NIV has the apostles saying 'We will turn this responsibility over to them' (Acts 6:3). If the apostles had been overseeing the distribution previously, but not very closely due to other pressures, this shows a mature and gracious reaction on their part to justified criticism.

5   It seems significant that whereas we find elders mentioned on their own in the New Testament (Acts 14:32; 20:17), deacons seem always to be referred to in conjunction with the office of elder, never separately (Philippians 1:1; 1 Timothy 3).

6   The qualifications for elders and deacons are very similar except that the elders must be 'able to teach'. It does not say

that the deacons must not teach, but simply that the elders *must have this gift.* This parallel of qualifications is obvious if the work of elders and deacons is so closely related.

7   There is little about the actual specific function of deacons in the New Testament, whereas there is a great deal about that of elders. Has the Holy Spirit left us to guess at the function of deacons? I think not. The deacons' work being part of the elders' work, having specified the elders' work, he has also outlined the sphere in which the deacons move.

Deacons then were the *general arm* of the eldership. They were entrusted with various jobs to relieve pressure on the elders, but were in the happy position of not holding ultimate responsibility. The buck does not stop with the deacons, but with the elders!

When in recent times churches began to appoint elders, there was a general understanding of a clear distinction between the work of elders and deacons. The elders did the spiritual work while the deacons dealt with the business of the church. This may perhaps be a rough guide but as we have seen is not entirely scriptural, and in practice it can lead to the impoverishment of the church. The Book of Acts seems to go out of its way to stress the fact that the 'proto-deacons' were spiritually very talented and gifted men. Philip was both a deacon and an evangelist (Acts 6:5; 8:5) while Stephen was involved in a ministry of 'great wonders and miraculous signs among the people'(Acts 6:8). The gifts and talents of deacons will be under-used if their work is restricted merely to areas of business and of physical needs. It may be helpful to a church for a deacon to be entrusted with a spiritual ministry while the elders' time is being totally swallowed up by some particularly tricky situation. Likewise it may be helpful for an elder to get his hands dirty and to be involved with the maintenance of the building, setting an example to the rest of the flock.

Sometimes there has developed an exclusive attitude between elders and deacons. 'You leave us to get on with our work and we will leave you to get on with yours.' This is entirely foreign to the atmosphere of the New Testament.

Most important of all there must be the closest possible

link of affection and confidence between elders and deacons.
It is a matter of vital importance. The warmth and mutual
regard in the relationship is seen by the rest of the flock and
will set an example to them. A 'them' and 'us' attitude can
only be destructive. A spirit of competition or even conflict
spells disaster.

(John Benton)

How is this to be translated into efficient church administration?
Again, flexibility is to be exercised, not only in the initial stages of
appointments being made, but as experience is gained and changes
of personnel take place.

There will be certain areas of work with which the elders will
deal and they will have separate meetings to discuss such things.
These will be mostly to do with the spiritual care of members, and
handling spiritual problems. The elders are always at liberty to ask
deacons or any other suitable people to assist them in given cases.
Likewise there will be work delegated to the deacons that they can
deal with, and they should be trusted to do so. If elders and deacons
always meet together one of the benefits of delegating duties to the
deacons is lost, namely, saving valuable time.

But the situation must not develop into two watertight compart-
ments and ways should be found to co-ordinate the work, avoid
duplication and crossed lines. Some churches have a system of
regular meetings of elders and deacons together. Others always
have an elder at deacons' meetings. In my own church the elders and
deacons and their wives have an 'away day' together, twice a year,
for prayer, to encourage one another, to iron out current problems
and to review the progress of the work as a whole.

Open fellowship between the leaders should be such that it is
impossible for one to subject the others to a surprise resignation.
Where understanding and mutual confidence grow, leaders become
aware of stresses and disaffections before they reach breaking point.

While in no way wishing to contradict what I have written, it may
be helpful to mention those areas of work that elders have often delegated to deacons. These are general administration, secretarial
work, finance, care of buildings, communication within the church
and on behalf of the church, and social welfare. There is no reason
at all why deacons should not share in regular pastoral visiting, leading house-groups, running bookstalls and many such ministries.

It is true the deacons' task is to relieve the elders of those things that distract them from 'prayer and the ministry of the Word' and oversight, but it is also true that elders should ensure the deacons are valued for their work. It is the privilege of deacons to focus and motivate the caring ministries of the whole church. The development of plural eldership should not result in a devaluation of the ministry of deacons, but rather release them to explore avenues of service not possible before for want of time. Furthermore, the spiritual qualifications of deacons underline the essential spiritual nature of the work delegated to them. There is a worldly approach to church finances, building repairs and administration that has to be rejected. All these things are to be done efficiently with spiritual grace, and with trust in the Lord. One treasurer with whom I have worked often dealt with a problem in this way. 'As treasurer with responsibility in this field I have to tell you that we do not have the money to finance this project. The cost would be this, and the shortfall would be that. I hope you clearly understand what I am saying. But now, as a member of this church, if the church believes we should do this thing I will support that decision without reserve.'

Questions

1 In your church, what is the best way for elders and deacons to relate to each other?
2 Are there people in your church who could assist either the elders or the deacons in their work?

20.
Leaders and ladies

I am sorry if the title of this chapter offends some but as the book is written from the standpoint of elders, it is the best I can do!

We must not approach this subject under the pressure of modern feminism, nor from the standpoint of traditional roles. Jesus Christ is Lord of both men and women, and of both husbands and wives, within the church. Scripture must therefore be our sole guide. But here there are problems of interpretation still very much under discussion among our theologians. We need to go as far as we can clearly see Scripture prescribes, but should beware of impetuosity based on speculative ideas as to the meaning of particular texts. We need also to avoid offence and division among the churches. In dealing with one aspect of this subject Paul wrote, 'If anyone wants to be contentious about this, we have no other practice — nor do the churches of God' (1 Corinthians 11:16).

The relationship between elders and deacons and their wives is a matter of considerable importance. It has the possibility of great blessing in the life of the church, but failure at this level will certainly be disastrous.

The teaching of Paul in Ephesians 5:22-33 sets the standard for this relationship. 'Wives submit to your husbands as to the Lord ... as the church submits to Christ so also wives should submit to their husbands in everything.' This submission is not servile nor is it the result of fear. Rather it is based on a mutual loving obedience to Jesus Christ.

'Husbands love your wives, just as Christ loved the church and gave himself for her ... husbands ought to love their wives as their own bodies.' It seems to me that the teaching here could not be clearer. As a mere man I have to say to any wives who chafe at this, 'Don't envy the role of your husband. The standard he is given is devastating in its challenge — pray for him!' And husbands, remember that while there is love in submission there is also submission in love.

This relationship of love and mutual respect between husbands and wives is first to be seen and felt in the home by those who visit. It is also to be seen and felt in the life of the church. If there are tensions and fundamental disagreements between leadership husbands and wives these can be felt by others and will undermine the unity of the church. All such matters need to be resolved in prayerful fellowship in the secret place of the home. Young people and unconverted people are often drawn to Christ by what they see in the relationship between the leaders and their wives. Visitors in the home find love and peace at a level they rarely if ever see among non-Christians.

Where there are children the atmosphere of love extends to the relationship of the parents with them, and as we have seen the management of their family by elders is an important test of their suitability. One aspect of this is the pressure on the relationship between the parents when church duties take one of them from the home many evenings in a week and this pressure can be very difficult to manage. If the husband is a leader in the church and as a consequence is frequently absent from the family, he must be very sensitive to the burden this places on his wife. There must be mutual support and encouragement and each must be willing to sacrifice the other's company for the Lord's sake and his church, but none of this should be taken for granted or allowed to go on unchecked.

It is the duty of the elders as a whole to be aware of these problems, and to try to ensure that family relationships are not unduly strained by excessive demands being made upon husband and wife, together or individually. It may be necessary temporarily to reduce the demands made on the time of a particular elder whose daily work and family commitments are especially heavy. Increasingly nowadays both husband and wife are in employment; this may be necessary to bring adequate money into the home or it may be the right use of gifts the Lord has given; but where for whatever reason, husband and wife are working, the demands of leadership in the church can become an even greater cause of stress. People in

administrative and executive positions are under particular pressure in the modern business world, and they are often the people in
church leadership. These things need to be understood.

What is the work of the wife of a leader in the church? The basis
of the husband and wife relationship as given in Genesis 2:18
extends to every part of their lives together. 'The Lord God said, It
is not good for the man to be alone, I will make a helper suitable for
him.' We understand then that a leader's wife should be seen to
encourage and support her husband, and help him in his work so far
as she can. Resenting late nights, despising the work the leaders do,
failure to pray for her husband, these things are no help, they dis-
honour the Lord. However, discerning comments on matters under
discussion, constructive criticism of the leaders' performance,
thoughtful suggestions about a matter being neglected or well done;
such things should be accepted gladly and are a great help. There is
a tradition that elders' business is very secret and is not to be shared
with others, even their wives. I believe there are very few items, if
any, that elders should not discuss privately with their wives. If an
elder has not sufficient discretion to know when absolute secrecy
has to be observed, I doubt if he should be an elder. If an elder's wife
has not the ability to keep quiet about matters shared with her by her
husband, again, I doubt if her husband should be an elder. The NIV
translation of 1 Timothy 3:11 is, 'in the same way their wives are to
be women worthy of respect, not malicious talkers, but temperate
and trustworthy in everything'. If in the context this is a reference
to deacons' wives, we can surely argue that it applies in practice to
elders' wives as well.

A further question arises. Is there a specific role for the wives of
leaders in the church apart from giving help to their husbands?
Traditionally the pastor's wife was expected to lead work among the
women, and often to take an active part in children's work and in
visiting homes. This was not necessarily because she was suitably
gifted, but because she was 'the pastor's wife'. In this context other
elders' or deacons' wives had no mould into which they were
expected to fit. More recently we have learnt to speak of 'the wife
of the pastor or elder' emphasising that she is first of all her
husband's wife like any other married lady. Also as we have already
mentioned, either by necessity or preference, elders' wives are
increasingly taking paid or voluntary work outside the direct service
of the church.

I think it is a good thing that the traditional mould is being broken. All too often wives were expected to fulfil a role for which they were not suited. As we have argued in the case of elders themselves, so with their wives or any other members of the church, the first consideration should be what gifts and talents the Lord has given. Like any other lady in the church a leader's wife should be able to exercise her abilities as far as possible in the life of the church. If this is not catered for, no one should be surprised if a leader's wife like any other member, may seek fulfilment in other spheres.

Whenever a tradition is broken there is the danger of important things being neglected. In the old pattern there was reasonable certainty that important work in the church would be done; now this may not be so certain. I would argue, therefore, that whenever possible the church should come first in the thinking of all concerned, even if this means less money coming into the home. But this applies to all members of the church, men and women. When roles are reversed in the home, the wife being the money earner, the husband may be released for work in the church for which he is suited. All this may be seen as part of the loving providence of God.

It is beyond the scope of this book to discuss the role of women in a local church in depth, but it is certainly an essential part of the elders' responsibility to ensure as far as possible that all the gifts and talents the Lord has given are used. A man should not do a certain job merely because he is a man. Likewise we must not be under feminist pressure to give women work simply to be in the fashion. If a woman is gifted in any way, that gift should be used if at all possible.

William Hendriksen translates 1 Timothy 3:11: 'Women similarly...' and argues that the reference is not to wives and that the women here are

> viewed as rendering special service in the church as do the elders and deacons. They are a group by themselves, not just wives of the deacons nor all the women who belong to the church. On the other hand the fact that no special or separate paragraph is used in describing their necessary qualifications, but that these are simply wedged in between the stipulated requirements for deacons with equal clarity, indicates that these women were not to be regarded as constituting a third office in the church, the

office of deaconesses, on a par with and endowed with equal authority to that of deacons ... As to Romans 16:1, 'Our sister Phoebe, a servant of the church' — no adequate reason has been given to prove that the term used in the original does not have its more usual meaning — servant.

(Commentary on Timothy and Titus).

We see then that there is good reason for women to be used in responsible ministries in the church. In many cases church leaders are suffering from stress not only because of the amount of work there is to do but because they are not using to the full the potential help among the women of the church. I see no reason why suitable women should not be invited to take part in elders' and deacons' meetings or that they should not have work delegated to them by those leaders. The elders have the overall and final responsibility before the Lord. Everything else, it seems to me, is a matter of the use of the right people in the right places, whether they are men or women.

The great aim should be for all to have a sense of being 'workers together with God'. This means there must be an absence of a superior spirit on the part of any. Paul referred to his colleagues as 'fellow-labourers' and expressed his appreciation of the work of both men and women (Romans 16:1-16; Philippians 2:25; 4:3; Colossians 4:11; Philemon 24). This was not an expression of condescension, it arose out of a genuine sense of the worth and usefulness of others in the team.

Questions

1 How can your church leaders ensure that their thinking genuinely takes into account the feminine view point?

2 Where the wife is the dominant partner in the marriage of a leader, how can Scriptural principles be honoured, and the wife is not frustrated?

21.
Counselling and discipline

We need to remind ourselves constantly that a local church does not exist in order merely to perpetuate itself as an institution. There must always be an objective and I suggest the following sums it up.

> The aim should be so to apply the truth, love and direction of Jesus Christ that the church becomes a Spirit-filled community within which the members grow in faith, hope and love and in likeness to Christ; being prepared for everlasting glory and reaching out with the gospel locally, in the country and throughout the world.

In my own church the elders and deacons summed up their task as 'growth to glory'.

We also need to be reminded of the kind of leadership the elders are to exercise which we discussed in chapters 12. Elders are never more nor less than servants of the church and this attitude must come through in all their dealings with the members. Here we will look at two aspects of ministry, personal counselling and discipline.

Personal counselling

Traditional pastors were expected to visit their members regularly. Very often such visits were times of spiritual fellowship and counselling; but all too frequently those men spent much time in calls which were little more than friendly occasions. There is every good reason for elders to meet church members at a social level in their homes or churches. Christians enjoy one another's company, but the main work of elders is at a spiritual level and it is a waste of their time for the emphasis to be on social calls. The whole church should be motivated to cater for the social aspect of fellowship among the members; they should be encouraged to meet each other and to help each other in physical and material ways. Such fellowship will often lead to spiritual help and encouragement, and this should be seen as harmonising with the ministry of the elders. Perhaps these contacts will expose hidden spiritual or material needs that should be referred to the leaders.

Visiting of members by elders should be a blend between regular calls and calls for specific purposes. Elders should be available to the church at all times. But here a problem has been encountered when a plural eldership has been established. When there was but one pastor everyone knew where to go for help — to the pastor for spiritual help or to the church secretary for just about everything else! Now where there is a group of elders and a group of deacons the membership can be confused. The great thing is for the problem to be recognised, then each church will work out its own answer. Some churches divide the membership into groups with an elder serving each group. Whatever arrangement is made it should be clear to all members whom they should consult on any given matter. If the leaders don't know their own allocation of responsibilities, they should not be surprised if the church is confused. The leaders must decide who is responsible for each aspect of need and that must be made clear to all members. The administration should be as simple as possible; the more complicated it is the more time will be wasted, and the confidence of members will be diminished.

Some preaching elders have set times when they are preparing their sermons, and when they are not available for consultation by members. There may be some situations where this is necessary. Temperaments differ among elders as in every other sphere of life; every elder must be persuaded for himself. For my part, I have always felt I wanted to be available to my people at all times. There was a price to pay but in this my conscience was most at ease.

One aspect of personal counselling fraught with danger is the way that some people are becoming dependent on it. They treat the elder as a kind of psychologist on whom they lean. Some elders are becoming over-burdened with people who return to them again and again with the same spiritual problem. I admit that some of these problems never seem to go away, and there has to be constant 'nursing' (1 Thessalonians 2:7); but the danger is that too many people develop reliance on the elder instead of confidence in the Lord. In some cases the problem arises because the regular preaching is not applied pastorally. Paul said, 'my message and my preaching were not with wise and persuasive words, but with a demonstration of the Spirit's power, so that your faith might not rest on men's wisdom but on God's power' (1 Corinthians 2:4-5). Elders must seek the Spirit's power so that their people are convinced and become strong in the Lord. If the Word is applied to the spiritual experience of believers in the preaching there is less demand for personal attention. Nevertheless preaching elders are also pastors and should be in constant touch with the members.

A large amount of time can be spent in seeking to lead enquirers to repentance and faith. As in so many things there are two extremes to avoid. One extreme is impatience and writing people off because they seem to make no progress. We should remember the patience the Lord had with us. Compassion for the lost will drive us to persist in our efforts to help them. The other extreme is to refuse to let people go and so give them time that could perhaps be better used. Like our Master (Mark 10:17-27), we must be faithful in presenting the gospel and its challenge and in seeking to persuade unconverted people to turn to Christ, but we must in the end be prepared to see them walk away.

> Though he had come 'running', the greedy youth also 'went away grieved'. The most hopeful prospects often disappoint those of us who can only 'look on the outward appearance'. Though evangelists often see only the first signs of interest in the gospel, pastors who do not move on in a few days observe the sad scene of seekers turning away. Our Lord used this instance to instruct disciples who would often experience a similar 'let down'.
>
> (*Today's Gospel*, Walter J Chantry, Banner of Truth)

There is a growing practice of subjecting members in counselling sessions to deep inner self-scrutiny. This is the so-called 'Inner Healing' ministry. It is true that elders should probe delicately to discover causes of spiritual ill-health in their flock; too often we have worked at a very superficial level; but there has to be respect for the personality of others. In a report in *Evangelical Times,* April 1990 we read,

> The counsellor will probe deep into the past life of the counsellee, seeking to uncover all the hurts and repressed emotions. The session is often very long and the counsellee's life is bared. One friend remarked that after a ten hour counselling session, he felt he had been emotionally raped.

This is an abuse of an elder's ministry. It can be safe-guarded by two checks. One, only the Lord can truly probe our inner life by his Spirit through the Word. Two, the Scriptures require us to examine ourselves, not other people. It is one thing to help other people in that exercise by asking pertinent questions, but it is quite another to put ideas into their minds and to subject them to the force of our own personality. In public ministry an elder will rightly apply the Word to many situations, leaving the Lord to work in the heart of each listener. In personal dealings rather more reticence has to be exercised.

We are becoming painfully aware of the impact on the church of the breakdown of morals in society. It is a sad fact that there has been a marked increase of sexual sins among spiritual leaders, even in evangelical churches. For this reason elders and others involved in counselling need to take great care about their personal involvement. 'If you think you are standing firm be careful that you don't fall' (1 Corinthians 10:12). Close encounters with young people and in situations where the sympathy of a man is evoked for a woman, or of a woman for a man, are to be guarded with care and much prayer. Where possible counselling is best done by people of the same sex as the person seeking help (see Titus 2:4) but even this is no guarantee of safety. Often it is wise for a counsellor to be accompanied by a colleague, but in such a case only one should do the work lest the person being interviewed should feel threatened or pressurised.

Sometimes a person in a particularly difficult or delicate situation will plead that the elder keeps what he is told in complete confidence. This is a very natural request but I believe it is wise if possible to avoid accepting it. Such confidence ties the hands of the elder and prevents him consulting others whose advice would be helpful or who have greater expertise in such cases. My approach would be something like this: 'I understand why you want me not to tell anyone else about whatever your problem is; and if you insist I will agree to keep your confidence. But I assume you want the best possible answer to your problem and, you see, it is possible I would know someone who would give me advice to help me to help you. I gladly promise to consult no-one without your permission, so please trust me to do what is best rather than tie my hands in this way.' Of course, if we are held to secrecy we must honour our pledge, but often this means we are not able to find the best solution to the problem.

Discipline

Elders must guide the church in situations requiring public rebuke or dismissal from the membership. We should think of discipline in a positive way in terms of Christian discipleship. Seen in this light discipline begins with orderliness in the church, clear leading by the elders and systematic biblical teaching on all aspects of Christian conduct including discipline itself. But when a member is guilty of conduct publicly dishonouring the Lord by defiantly disobeying his rule, the elders must not shrink from disciplinary action.

The need for such action may arise in one of two ways. In the first, there may be a dispute between two members (Matthew 18:15-20) which they have not been able to resolve. An attempt has been made to do so on a personal level, and by involving one or two other members. But when all this has failed, and not till then, the elders will be called in to deal with the situation.

The second way the need for discipline may arise is the development of a problem with a member that is obvious to all. The New Testament does not provide us with exact procedures for the discipline of those who have greatly offended the Lord and dishonoured his church, but it is in harmony with the tenor of the Scriptures that prayer, time, patience and love should be given before any member is dismissed. No two cases are alike even if they appear to be so. All the circumstances of the offender should be taken into consideration. There should be instruction, exhortation and appeal made with a view to repentance and restoration. The Lord is dishonoured if the member is dealt with unjustly. For this reason it may be good for one or two elders to be appointed specifically to act as advocates for the person concerned. The Lord is dishonoured if the offender is not bathed in the love and prayers of the church. But the Lord is also dishonoured if the church refuses to take proper disciplinary measures (1 Cor. 5:2-6).

Some argue for three stages of disciplinary action. First, admonition; second, if admonition fails, suspension from the privileges of membership; third, if suspension does not produce repentance, the final act of excommunication.

I am not entirely satisfied with this, although it is a tidy method and has been common practice. The relevant Scriptures are: 2 Thessalonians 3:6-7; 10-11; 14-15; Matthew 18:17; 1 Corinthians 5; 1 Timothy 1:19-20; Titus 3:10. There are three main reasons for my unease. One is that to exclude someone from the privileges of membership such as the Lord's Supper as a second stage of discipline, deprives that person of the very ministry needed. Secondly, I am not happy about separating the Lord's Supper from membership. If we are members we should have access to the communion table. An offender may need to be suspended from some forms of service while he or she is under admonition (first stage). For example, it would be impossible for a Bible Class teacher to minister effectively in such circumstances. But it seems to me that every spiritual ministry should be available to a person so long as he or she is a member of the church. Thirdly, I believe the whole notion of excommunication is absent from the New Testament. Excommunication owes more to ecclesiastical tradition than to biblical teaching. In the New Testament people were either church members or they were not. The ultimate discipline was dismissal from the fellowship of the church which included the privileges of the Lord's Supper, and the 'felt' pleasure of the fellowship. We find no rules of dismissal in Scripture that relate directly to the communion service, only to the membership of the church. Therefore I see two stages only — first, loving, patient admonition frequently given, during which there is possible withdrawal from service but not from the privileges of the fellowship and its ministry. Second, dismissal from the membership, and therefore from all its privileges, but not from the congregation except in extreme cases of unruliness. Every church must draw its own conclusions in these things.

One thing is certain, dismissal from membership does not mean the person is declared to be a non-believer. Only the Lord knows those who are his (2 Timothy 2:19); but it does declare that this person is at best an unruly believer, but may prove not to be a believer in the last day. When this action is taken the offender is to be treated as a pagan (Matthew 18:17). But how should we treat a pagan? Surely with love and with constant prayer and effort towards his or her conversion. There is never a case for harshly writing a person off and refusing any further contact. There is always a case for seeking the restoration of those who have strayed from the Lord and his people. Paul's instructions to the Corinthian church included being ready to receive the offender back (2 Cor. 2:5-11).

When members leave a church because they are disaffected for some reason, the church does not merely receive a resignation, but positively dismisses such a person. When this happens the elders should subject the church to honest self-examination. Has the church failed this member through lack of love, patience, exhortation, or ministry? Does this departure expose a defect in the life of the church, in the preaching or in the fellowship, that needs to be put right?

Elders should be careful not to undermine the discipline of other local churches by receiving into membership those whom others have dismissed. It is always possible that such people have been dealt with unfairly. But there should be very careful investigation before conclusions are reached and the person concerned may need to be tested over a period of time before being accepted into membership.

Questions

1 How can an elder avoid members trusting in him and not in the Lord?
2 How can an elder 'shepherd the flock' from the pulpit without publicly 'getting at' individual people?

22.
Church business meetings

The church business meeting should not be any less of a spiritual experience than the prayer meeting or the Lord's Supper. A spiritual tone is often lacking because the meeting is conducted in a rigid manner following strict committee procedures, or it is not conducted in the context of prayer and worship and under the conscious lordship of Jesus Christ. The result is that members sometimes speak without submission and without love; the aim is to win a personal point of view rather than seeking the Lord's will. There is great need of prayer, love and submission on the part of leaders and members.

Churches determine their policy at gatherings known as church meetings. Here the membership gathers to uphold and proclaim the government of the church by our Lord Jesus Christ. At a church meeting, a church seeks to discover God's will for itself by prayer and submission to God's Word, and also prays for power and perseverance to do that will.

(*We Believe* — page 87)

This approach to a church business meeting requires a blend of efficiency with spiritual sensitivity permeated with love and prayer.

The full-time preaching elder is not necessarily the best person to conduct a church business meeting. Very often he is totally unsuitable and so just muddles along to the confusion of the church, when others present could do much better. But plural eldership does not mean the elders must follow a rota to conduct meetings of the church, much less the business meeting. The aim should be for the best people to lead meetings. In the case of a business meeting the most suitable person may not be an elder at all, but a spiritually minded member with the appropriate gift. This would not rob the elders of their oversight, but rather enable them to exercise it in a helpful atmosphere. This does not exclude the need for some less gifted members to be encouraged and to be used occasionally, nor giving opportunities by way of training and the discovery of hidden talents. Aiming for the best must include some flexibility—nothing is worse than a rigid adherence to one man or to a rota when it means that the least able person conducts a meeting of considerable delicacy or importance.

It is not necessary nor even desirable for one person to introduce every item on the agenda. The person responsible for the aspect of work to be reported on or discussed is most often the best person to open the subject to the meeting.

Elders should determine the agenda for a business meeting. Items for discussion should be with the aim of embracing the whole church in its spiritual progress. It is worth observing the specific reasons why local churches gathered in New Testament days, and the quotations noted in *We Believe* (pages 87-88);

Acts 1:15-26	The replacement of an apostle
2:1	Waiting on the Lord
6:2-6	Setting aside men for special administration
11:22	Providing for inter-church fellowship
13:1	The ministry of the Word
13:2, 3	The sending of missionaries
14:27	Rehearsing God's mighty acts
15:1-29	The defence and confirmation of the gospel
15:30-31	Receiving communications from brethren
1 Cor. 5:1-5	The discipline of offenders
(also Matthew 18:15-20)	
1 Cor. 11:17-34	Observing the Lord's Supper
14:26	The exercise of spiritual gifts
2 Cor. 8:19	To deal with monetary gifts
Col. 4:16	The reading of the Word
(also 1 Thessalonians 5:27)	

The above passages indicate that the church meeting is warranted and required by Scripture. The scriptures also suggest a number of guidelines for the conduct of church meetings. It is evident that the whole church should be gathered, and all members should make every endeavour to be present. For convenience we may distinguish between meetings for business and those for spiritual matters, but there is no fundamental difference between them. *Business meetings are also spiritual meetings.* The spirit of prayer and worship should pervade them all. As the matters discussed have to do with eternal issues, it is good to remember the Lord's abiding promise that where his church is gathered in his Name, he is in the midst. The whole church should be concerned in dealing with the defence of the truth, the ordering of worship, the appointment of elders and deacons, the sending out of missionaries, evangelistic problems and projects and the discipline of disorderly members. Routine matters such as finance, the maintenance of buildings etc. should be dealt with by the deacons without the need of referring details to the church for decisions. Nevertheless, reports of such matters should be given regularly so that all may be seen to be honestly conducted, not only before God but before men.

(Matthew 18:20; Acts 13:3; 2 Corinthians 8:21)

We have already stressed that the object of decision making is not to discover the majority opinion but to discern the mind of the Lord. The scriptures are the authority and the duty of the elders is to ensure submission to that authority. When matters under discussion cannot be resolved by reference to specific scriptures, the elders will need to explain the relevant biblical principles, and advise how these principles can be applied to the situation.

Some churches will prefer to adopt a system of voting to arrive at conclusions. This has the advantage that people are familiar with it in other spheres of life; it is the way we make decisions in our society. We may argue that the Scriptures are flexible on this matter and are capable of being adapted to the normal habits of any culture.

I do not wish to reject that way of approach completely but I think we must ask why the Lord in his providence established the early churches at a certain time in history, and in which there was no system of voting provided for. I believe there are good reasons for this. Experience teaches us that when a vote has been taken the effect is often to harden the minority in their opposition, or at least to leave them with feelings of grievance and failure. Division is created because the minority may genuinely believe the decision is dishonouring to the Lord and therefore harmful for the church. And then sometimes the leadership will be afraid of offending the minority, so they do not act on the decision. The result is that the church is ruled not by the Lord through elders but by a disaffected but influential minority. On the other hand it is self-evident that the majority are not always right.

We need to take seriously that the Holy Spirit can lead a church to unanimity of mind as well as heart (Acts 4:32; Philippians 2:2). This requires members and leaders alike to be submissive to the Spirit and to each other. Voting can be a substitute for true spirituality and Christlikeness in the whole church. This is needed if the elders are patiently to lead the church to a common mind. It may seem impossible but where it is aimed for the effect on the whole life of the church is profound.

Some matters can be reported on, opportunity given for questions and a general assent taken without making heavy weather of procedures or the formality of voting. A good chairman will sense unease in the church and discover the reasons for it. The problem may be cleared up immediately by a flexible approach but if there is serious questioning the elders must be prepared to postpone a decision. This will give time for further consideration, discussion and prayer with those who are troubled.

This process may seem rather tedious and time consuming but normally it is the best. There are occasionally situations in which elders must make decisions and act quickly before they can consult a church meeting. You don't hold a consultation if a blind man is walking towards the edge of a cliff! When immediate decisions have to be made, happy are the elders who can rely on the love and understanding of the church, even if with hindsight their actions prove to have been wrong. But there are very few matters so urgent that immediate decisions and actions have to be taken.

When a subject of major importance is due to be brought to the church there is a great danger that the elders will come to their conclusions, present them to the church, and expect the members to accept the recommendations. I say this is a danger, because the impression then given to the church is that there is nothing left for them to say, and the complaint 'we are only rubber stamps' will have some justification. A better procedure is for the church to be notified that the elders are about to discuss a certain issue, say, 'Where are we going as a church?' or, 'Should we have an evangelistic mission next year?' The church is asked to consider certain specific scriptures or practical questions and opportunity given for a free airing of ideas and views before the elders discuss the matter in any depth. The church will then have been involved in the matter from the beginning, and the leaders will have the benefit of all that the members have said.

In the long run, this procedure also has the advantage of saving time. The elders must give serious consideration to all that is said. Indeed, elders should feel free to invite any member to their discussions, particularly if such a member has specialist knowledge of the subject in hand, or strong views based on experience. Not only so, we should be grateful that the Lord sometimes gives light to the least likely member and this should keep the elders humble. Elders only earn the trust of the members if they are seen to take them seriously. Elders can show this in the way they present their conclusions to the church. 'We considered this suggestion for a long time and for these reasons we think it is a good idea (or not a good idea).' They must also still be willing patiently and prayerfully to think again in the light of discussion on their proposals. One advantage of a 'no voting' system is that one member with a good case to make, or a good idea to suggest, may be instrumental in a rethink by the elders and perhaps a modification of their recommendation.

We are unnecessarily fearful of a clash of opinion in a business meeting, and elders tend to work to avoid it at all costs, but the cost may be too high; because the exercise of expressing different views is one means of preventing an undercurrent of discontent, and of stimulating spiritual growth. This is not a case of agreeing to differ, but of a willingness to submit to one another in seeking the Lord's mind. By this means members grow in deeper love, patience and humility as they learn from one another.

None of this implies that elders merely edit the opinions of the members. It does mean they are acting as servants of the church, willing to submit patiently to the needs of the members. Good shepherds ensure the sheep are following closely. Elders are not a college of cardinals, but in the end elders will never allow themselves to be pressurised into presenting to the church conclusions which are in their view unbiblical or unwise.

When this kind of procedure has been followed a vote should not be necessary, but a 'show of hands' might be used to confirm the overwhelming conviction that the Lord has led the church to these conclusions. In these circumstances I do not believe it is necessary to ask 'Any against?' If there are those who are still not happy the procedure will already have brought that to light. The assumption must be that these people will support the decision because they are happy at least that their position has been thoroughly considered.

There will always be members who keep silent. If they disagree with the recommendations being made they do not make their unease known either in the church meetings or privately to the elders. Given a vote they will vote against the proposition or abstain. This is another reason why voting is unsatisfactory. The direction of the church should not be allowed to be affected by contrary votes or abstentions for which the reasons are not known. The silence of these members means that there has been no opportunity to minister to them or for their ideas to be seriously discussed by the elders; if they remain silent that is the only contribution that they can make to the proceedings however unsatisfactory this may be.

The aim should be unanimity. Whatever system is adopted it is not always possible for the ideal to be achieved. Where people are known to disagree with decisions that have been made, for whatever reason, care should be taken to minister positively to them. Riding rough shod over minorities is not part of the life of a church where the spirit of Jesus Christ prevails.

Questions

1   How could you make the headship of Christ more meaningful in your church business meeting?
2   Is unanimity in everything possible? If not, why not?

23.
Balanced church life

It is the responsibility of the elders to provide for all that is required of a church by the New Testament.

One of the most difficult things to maintain in both one's personal Christian life and church life is balance. There seems to be a tendency in many people to live either at one end of the pendulum swing, or at the other. All of us are tempted at times to live by reaction rather than by action. If we're not careful, we react against erroneous positions of our own or of others and swing out to the opposite extreme.

Some Christian writers have taken note of this difficulty of maintaining balance. J. C. Ryle warns us that 'there is a constant tendency in the human mind to run to extremes'. John R. W. Stott considers this area one of Satanic attack when he says that '...one of the greatest weaknesses which we as Christians (especially evangelical Christians) display is our tendency to extreme or imbalance. It seems there is almost no pastime the devil enjoys °more than tipping Christians off balance.' What is true of individual Christians is also true of churches. When our churches are lopsided, unbalanced, and out of proportion, we misrepresent both the message we preach and the Master we serve. We also mislead the sheep who look to us for guidance.

(Stuart B Latimer — *Shepherding God's flock,* page 63
Sprinkle Publications)

There should be balance of intake and output. A church where worship, fellowship and teaching prevail without an evangelistic thrust will be like a body suffering from an unbalanced diet and too little exercise, getting nowhere. There are dangers in emphasising any one of these four aspects above the others. All fellowship without worship will lead to an experience-centred rather than a God-centred church. All teaching and no fellowship will lead to a cold, academic atmosphere with little love toward God, other Christians or unbelievers. Evangelism without teaching will be superficial, without fellowship it will lack context, and without worship it will lack true objective.

Fellowship should be both practical and spiritual. At the practical level it involves members caring for each other in their material and physical needs. At the spiritual level it includes testimony, prayer, exhortation and encouragement. Teaching should cater for the needs of a wide range of age and experience. Teaching fails in its objective if it does not include application to every part of human life. Evangelism needs to reach different kinds of people. It should especially distinguish, as did our Lord and the apostles, between the approach appropriate to those who know the Scriptures, and those who have no knowledge of spiritual things.

Balance in worship

We worship a Triune God, Father, Son and Holy Spirit, and due praise and adoration should be given to all three Persons. Balanced worship will include instruction, exaltation, meditation, prayer and exhortation, all in a gospel context.

There should be a balance between orderliness and liberty. The Scriptures require everything to be 'done in a fitting and orderly way' (1 Corinthians 14:40). These words occur in a passage correcting unruliness in the worship of the Corinthian church. Elders must see that there is not chaos, flippancy, clumsy informality or anything that detracts from the seriousness of worship or the power of the message. But this can be taken too far producing an atmosphere heavy with solemnity in which the joy of the Lord is crushed out. The same apostle who wrote 1 Corinthians 14:40 also wrote: 'Do not put out the Spirit's fire' (1 Thessalonians 5:19). This is not the same thing as excitement worked up by endless singing; it is not manipulation of the emotions. But the gospel preached in the power of the Spirit will move a congregation to exaltation. We must not be so respectable as to despise tears of repentance or expressions of joy in the Lord. We must not exclude the possibility that the Spirit may break into our planned service in unusual ways. The preacher may be redirected in his message, or the congregation may break out into singing. There was a time when congregational participation in worship was rare. Now we have times of prayer, testimonies, music groups, and other forms of mutual ministry, and there is the danger of worship and of preaching being crowded out. The Spirit is not the author of confusion (1 Corinthians 14:33) but he is the giver of exuberant spiritual life.

Groups within the church

The oversight of the elders concerns the whole life of the church. When this has not been so, youth organisations, home groups, women's fellowships, children's meetings, and other groups have sometimes operated apart from the church. They have even been known to develop opposition to the church. Also there is the danger of imbalance when one group absorbs time and resources in a way that cramps the work of others.

Even in the happiest situations 'if you think you are standing firm, be careful that you don't fall' (1 Corinthians 10:12). It is better to establish safeguards against problems than to be compelled to face them when they arise. The first safeguard is to ensure if possible that an elder is recognised for each part of the work. He will have free access to the meetings of the leaders and of the group itself, without imposing a rigid rule upon it or stifling initiative. The elder should make sure that regular reports of the work are made to the eldership and to the church. Group leaders must be willing to receive guidance and accept correction. The second safeguard is that the leaders, and all responsible for teaching should be in harmony with the theological stance of the church, and they should regularly receive teaching within the church. It is a good idea occasionally to call a meeting of all group leaders for prayer and fellowship, to clarify their relationships with each other and with the church, and to underline their responsibility to the church. At the same time elders should remind members of their duty to support and to pray for the various groups within the church.

Care needs to be taken to ensure that the members are not so busy in group work that they have no time for their personal prayer and family life or they are not able regularly to attend church meetings for prayer, Bible study and fellowship.

Balance in coping with traditionalism

We need a balance between going on as we always have done, and making changes for the sake of them. Every church gathers traditions. Some are longstanding reaching back many decades. But as soon as a new church is founded it also begins to form traditions of its own. A leader of a young church in America said to me, 'I wish it would be possible for us to begin all over again after twenty five years.' He knew how easily certain attitudes, auxiliaries, and methods of approach can be set in concrete, any change is thought to be a departure from Scripture.

There are good, bad and indifferent traditions. Paul wrote about traditions (1 Corinthians 11:2; 2 Thessalonians 2:15; 3:6; 'teachings' = 'traditions' NIV Margin), and elders must see that the church follows such apostolic traditions. Apart from this, traditions arise in a number of ways.

a   Things into which the church has drifted without thought or biblical testing, (e.g. jumble sales for church funds; children always being kept out of services).

b   Things that arose from what was believed to be a clear understanding of Scripture, (e.g. preaching central to services; special instruction classes for those who are to become church members).

c   Things that were fashionable at the time the practice began, (e.g. standing for the benediction; organs).

d   Things that arose from the culture of the area, (e.g. Harvest festivals; taking votes at church meetings).

e   Things that attempted to answer specific problems, (e.g. Sunday schools; a minimum age for church members).

I am not arguing that any of these examples are right or wrong. An examination in the light of Scripture may justify them or it may not. The great thing is that the life and traditions of the church should not be taken for granted, but there should be a willingness to change either because of further light from Scripture or because circumstances have changed and new challenges demand new approaches. Beware of personal preferences, bright ideas, fashions, group pressures and what succeeded in previous churches. But how should elders deal with resistance in the church to reformation or change?

I suggest that nothing is done until the prayer life of the church is strong and the members are praying for the Lord to lead the church by his Word. An attitude of mind needs to be developed in which members become accustomed to submitting everything to Scripture.

If the church is being led by a man called from another church, a lot will depend on the terms of his acceptance of that position. If he was wise he secured an agreement that all things at all times would be submitted to the Lord's will revealed in Scripture. If this was done, the church should be prepared sooner or later for some of its traditions to be challenged.

We should resist the temptation to make too many changes too quickly. We need to determine priorities by asking, Is there a tradition that is hindering the growth of the church spiritually and numerically? This then will be the matter to put before the Lord for his guidance and help in seeking change. At the same time steps can be taken to prepare the church; teaching can be given from the relevant Scriptures without necessarily spelling out immediately the full implications for the church as seen by the elders.

I shall always be grateful to the Lord for leading me to give an extended series of Bible studies under the title 'What is a New Testament church?' before recommending certain changes in a church where I have been privileged to serve.

When adequate time has been given for prayer and Bible teaching, the matter needs to be presented to the church sympathetically, graciously and clearly. So often members get wrong ideas about the proposed change because it is entirely new to them, because of some past unfortunate experience, or because they have not understood.

Elders may need to be sensitive to the effects of changes on individual members. It may be their family life will be disturbed, or habits of a lifetime will be disrupted. We need to be especially sensitive to people who have been leaders in a part of the work which is now to be disbanded and to make sure that they are not left out on a limb. Opposition to changes on the basis of sheer selfishness, unconcern for opportunities and for the good of the church should be firmly resisted.

After the change has been proposed time must be given for prayer, questions and discussion. Patience is essential. Remember that for some people their tradition is their stability and if you take it away from them they are all at sea. Change is unhealthy if it results in dishonouring the Lord or destroying the fellowship. It is better to seek progress within a traditional structure than to destroy the unity of the church. Healthy change can only be achieved through much prayer, much patience and the working of the Holy Spirit.

Balance in commitment

A church may have no more activity than Sunday services and a mid-week meeting, plus children's meetings and youth work. But even at this level of demand members often feel pressurised. Elders need to be sensitive to changes in the working conditions of many members. Michael Bentley in a paper read at a ministers' fraternal in January 1988 drew attention to this:

Many churches are beginning to suffer because more and more firms are demanding that their employees be prepared to work for long periods outside of the old 9-5 bracket. Nurses and other shift workers have always had to take turns at working on Sundays and week evenings. We are used to these people missing prayer meetings and Sunday services; but now executives and others are being called upon to work late in the evening, bring urgent work home with them, and work on Saturdays and Sundays when their firms demand it. Even if companies do not ask their employees to work late, they often give them such a workload with short deadlines, that they have to work many extra hours to get it done on time. They are often faced with going to the prayer meeting and working into the early hours of the morning, or staying away from church to do their work so that they can get to bed at a reasonable time. More people now find they are unable to attend the mid-week meeting because of the increasing pressures of working life. Here are some of them:

Some are studying for professional examinations, and to get the promotion they need, they must give many hours of spare time to their studies.

Some are school teachers, and they have more lessons to prepare and assignments to mark.

Some have extra evening meetings to attend in connection with their work.

For some their working day entails travelling very long distances (in this country and to the Continent) to other firms to attend conferences and consultations. They often do not get home until 9 pm. or later.

Some are so stressed at work that they are 'clapped out' when they do arrive home and they are either unable to get to the prayer meeting or if they do attend, they go to sleep in the Bible study!

Some pastors are getting worried because, on occasions, even keen church members absent themselves from the Sunday evening service. The old idea of Mum and Dad taking it in turns to go to church while the other one stays at home, is beginning to die out. Why is this? It is because on week-days some men leave home before their children are up in the morning and they arrive back home long after their children have gone to bed. If the children are young then Sunday evening is the last opportunity for families to spend time together 'as a family' until the following Saturday.

Full-time elders may not always realise how much unreasonable pressure they are putting on their members, especially when they are leaders of group activities. Ideally all members should be at all church gatherings, not because of a rule written or assumed, but for their own spiritual health and the good of the church as a whole. But there must be flexibility in expectation and in these days we may need to reduce the amount of activity and so not to make unbearable demands in terms of attendance at meetings. Often Sunday is by no means a day of rest and there needs to be constant review of the 'programme' of the church.

Questions

1 What traditions in your church are a hindrance to progress?
2 Are the members of your church over-worked, or are they under-used because of their lack of commitment?

24.
Preachers and preaching

Preaching is essential to the life of a church and elders must ensure the church is well served with the ministry of the Word.

Preaching elders need constantly to examine themselves. They must have a zeal for God's glory, zeal for God's truth, zeal for the welfare of the church, and for the salvation of sinners. Like their Master they should be able to say, 'Zeal for your house will consume me' (John 2:17). Stimulation for such zeal will be found in prayer and meditation, the Scriptures, fellowship, visiting the people, and a broad range of reading, and this will be the context within which sermons are born.

Where do sermons come from? We should avoid hobby-horses to please ourselves, and rather have the needs of the people in our minds. What is the condition of the church? What are the worries and burdens of the people? What are the spiritual conflicts of the hour? What doctrines have been neglected or not adequately understood? How can we equip believers to witness to others? How can we present the gospel yet more clearly? These are the issues we should seek to address. Continuing with a series of expositions may not meet the greatest need; we must be willing to change direction or to break off from something we ourselves have been enjoying. New light on a text, a brilliant thought in our reading, an interesting way of dividing a text, none of these things will of necessity be the Lord's direction. Nevertheless they may be the means God uses to give us a message for the hour. Whatever else we do our selection of subject must be with a view to preaching Christ. All preaching should be in the context of the gospel and in dependence on the Holy Spirit.

Preaching must be relevant, this means the timeless message of Scripture is to be understandable to people of our own day. It also means showing how the message relates to modern life; we must think with twentieth century minds and speak in harmony with a twentieth century context. We don't use 'sickles' now, we use combine harvesters. For a very high proportion of our families in any town divorce is the norm. Many children have a jaundiced view of what a father is. Relevance also means that we don't fight yesterday's battles in the theological, social and scientific fields. The truth of God itself is unchanged and unchanging, but even within Scripture the language, arguments and illustrations move on with the centuries. Our Lord and his apostles spoke Old Testament truth in New Testament terms.

But even relevance is not enough. We can be relevant but not significant. Our hearers must be made to realise that the message has a significant meaning to them personally, and that there is clear direction as to what they must do. In the end it is not the twentieth century that matters, but an individual conscience in the presence of a holy God of love.

We must work at the application of the message. I was trained in the school of — introduction, headings and divisions, conclusion. This may be good for lecturing, but it is bad for preaching. In preaching application should be made throughout the sermon even if there is a further concentration of it at the end; and even then we should not be concluding an oration but applying a message. In many ways application is the hardest and yet most important part of the sermon. What is in the passage that throws light on world problems that worry our people — that will help them to grow spiritually and in their witness to unconverted people — that will challenge the unconverted in a new way?

This ministry has to be sound in doctrine and Bible-based in its presentation. I am persuaded that regular Bible exposition is the best way to ensure a good spiritual diet, nevertheless sermons should be varied in style. Two sermons on Sunday and a mid-week Bible study all in the style of verse by verse exposition of the text of Scripture may be satisfying to the preacher, but will very likely be tedious to the congregation and will certainly fail to provide a balanced understanding of the truth and its application to life. There should be some text by text exposition but a preacher should also deal with whole passages, or whole books of the Bible; he should take up topics of passing concern to the people; he should also deal with

specific problems of the Christian life, and also present arguments
for the truth of the Bible and the Christian faith.

The present generation of preachers, whether it knows it or not,
has been greatly influenced by the publication of Dr. Martyn Lloyd
Jones' sermons on the letters by Paul to the Romans and to the
Ephesians. Among many others I am profoundly grateful for 'the
Dr.' and his expository method. But I recommend a careful comparison between his word by word treatment of Romans and
Ephesians, with his thematic approach to John 17 (four volumes
published by Kingsway) or his *Revival* (published by Marshall
Pickering), and his evangelistic apologetic approach on 2 Timothy
1 (*I am not ashamed,* published by Hodder), or his *Sandfield sermons* (Banner of Truth Trust). Dr. Lloyd Jones was a long way from
using the same approach all the time.

Care must also be taken to present a balanced view of the
Christian life. There is law and liberty; looking back, looking in,
looking on, and looking out; both faith and works, both trusting and
trying, both resting and wrestling, and both separation and
involvement.

I am aware that some people feel that the ministry in the church
gatherings should be teaching for the church, while evangelistic
preaching is for outside the church orbit. I respect that view so long
as the evangelism is genuinely catered for with at least as much
effort as the in-church ministry. For my part I believe all our
preaching should be in a gospel context. If members bring
unconverted friends to services they should have confidence that the
preaching will be understandable mentally, trusting the Lord to
open minds spiritually. This is not to say that our preaching should
constantly deal with the great themes of sin and salvation.
Unconverted people need to see that Christianity is not a sideline,
but embraces the whole of life, nothing excluded.

Preaching will be ineffective if it is not understood by people
who are unfamiliar with the puritan books of theology or specialist
evangelical language. I am persuaded there are biblical words that
cannot be replaced by any others but I am equally persuaded that
preachers should more frequently realise that their business is to
explain those terms. For example, words like justification and
sanctification are 'shorthand' for very great concepts, and preachers
must not complain of lack of response if they do not take the trouble
to use the 'long hand', spelling out frequently the gospel implicit in

those words. One reason why members are often not able to communicate the gospel intelligently to their friends is that they are not shown how to do it by their preaching elders. I do believe the Holy Spirit alone can regenerate a sinner, but I do not believe we should rely on the Spirit to perform a second miracle by translating our words into plain English enabling our hearers to understand. Thank God he does so at times, but that is because he is gracious and not because he endorses our laziness.

Preaching can also be ineffective because it lacks warmth and fervency. Our preaching should have order; people should be able to follow us from one thought to another; if they can't we will lose their attention and they will 'switch off'. But even more important is love, feeling and conviction. Preaching is not the same as Bible study; the latter can assume that the congregation wants to explore deeper truths of the Scriptures. Preaching is a popular presentation of the truth of the gospel designed to command a hearing and, by the Spirit, to produce conviction and response. Preaching should be animated, designed to capture the ears and the hearts of the congregation.

Why do we fail to gain the attention not just of any unbelievers present, not just of those 'awkward' teenagers, but sometimes even of the 'dear saints of God'? The problem is not, of course, with the message, for 'God was pleased through the foolishness of what was preached to save those who believe' (1 Corinthians 1:21); so perhaps it lies with the thoughtlessness of the preacher who has simply not taken enough time to consider the best medium through which to convey his message.

In saying this, warning bells immediately begin to sound, for preachers should never become pulpiteers, or professionals (in the worst sense of the word) who use every emotional artifice, secular gimmick or even gratuitous 'humour' in order to gain attention. But if we may not borrow from the impressive but empty oratory of a Demosthenes, or from the slick presentation of a Saatchi and Saatchi, we still have much to learn from a Hosea!

The prophet Hosea speaks to every generation as a wonderful combination of 'heat' and 'light' in his message directed at the 'covenant complacency' of Israel. While the

grounds for their complacency were very different from that
of western man in the twentieth century the fact of their
complacency (and the resulting hardness of heart) was the
same — as was the shaky foundation on which that complacency was built. If Hosea's words fell upon his generation
like a sledgehammer, at least he was aiming to crack more
than a nut! And if he could be so vivid, almost violent at times
in his choice of language, how can we justify the 'cold fish'
approach? Vivid, of course, is an understatement for much of
Hosea's language. His words demand attention, even when
doing no more than describing an actual situation (or making
a prediction), without recourse to simile, metaphor, extended
illustration, historical allusion, or those wonderful purple
passages where metaphors are so mixed as to make the purist
despair, but his hearers sit bolt upright!

(Clifford Bailey, *Foundations,* Autumn 1990)

Animation and conviction are not to be theatrical, put on for
impression, but they are to arise from the Holy Spirit's fire in the
heart (Jeremiah 20:9) and from a sense of thrill with the message
being proclaimed.

We should also be urgent in preaching, conveying the importance of what we are saying. Those who are familiar with the
sermons of Dr. Martyn Lloyd Jones have often been amused at the
frequency with which he said something like: 'Nothing is more
important for us in these days than...' or, 'I am willing to assert that
the greatest need of people today is...' In the Doctor's mind what he
preached now was the most vital thing in the world. No wonder
people listened to what he said.

I believe provision should be made for our congregation to say
if they have understood our preaching, and what they understood us
to say. Jesus once asked his disciples at the end of a sermon: 'Have
you understood these things?' (Matthew 13:51). If our Lord thought
it wise to ask that question it must surely be important for us to do
so. Any preacher who has exposed himself in this way will know
that it can be a very humbling experience. Some of my most
challenging and yet rewarding experiences have been when I have
gathered the people after a service and asked them to tell me what
they had understood me to say, what they had not understood, and
how they would apply the message to themselves. The truth is that

much of our preaching is either not understood or is misunderstood, and the fault is not that of the congregation but of the preacher. Good teaching must involve the opportunity for questions to be asked for clarification and for proof of what we have said.

Good preaching also begins with a concern for the specific needs of the people. This observation by Dr. Lloyd Jones may surprise some who have a wrong conception of his approach to preaching:

> I am not and have never been a typical Welsh preacher. I felt that in preaching the first thing that you had to do was to demonstrate to the people that what you were going to do was very relevant and urgently important. The Welsh style of preaching started with a verse and the preacher then told you the connection and analysed the words, but the man of the world did not know what he was talking about and was not interested. I started with the man whom I wanted to listen, the patient. It was a medical approach really — here is a patient, a person in trouble, an ignorant man who has been to quacks, and so I deal with all that in the introduction. I wanted to get the listener and then come to my exposition. They started with their exposition and ended with a bit of application.
> (*The first forty years* by Iain H. Murray, pages 146/7)

So we see that the first two minutes of a sermon are vital. If we have not captured the ears of the people by then we do not deserve they should listen to us any further. Many of our loyal people will bear with us, bless them! But we will not build our congregation with new people if we are careless of basic principles of communication. This does not mean our introduction should be lengthy. In the normal way it should be sufficient to show the importance of the subject and the need for people to listen to it. I doubt if a lengthy introduction showing the context or the historical and geographical background to the passage in hand will grab the ears of more than a few people in the congregation. Such matters should have been taken into account in the preparation so that the sermon has authority. They can also be embraced in the course of the message. We are not preaching a sermon simply to satisfy ourselves, but delivering a message to meet spiritual need and to feed hungry souls.

Our Lord said, 'Every teacher of the law who has been instructed about the kingdom of heaven is like the owner of a house who brings

out of his storeroom new treasures as well as old' (Matthew 13:52).
A preacher can be in bondage to the idea that he must always
produce something new; freshness is always desirable. When he
makes new discoveries of truth in the Word and presents them with
enthusiasm in his sermon this will come over well to the people.
What is new to us will give us a lively approach, but we must not be
held in slavery to newness. Our people need constantly reminding
of basic truth (see 2 Peter 1:12). With young people growing into
maturity, new people coming in, or long standing members who
need reminding, group leaders who need to be kept fresh in biblical
doctrine, elders should make sure that the church has reviewed the
whole scope of basic doctrine at least once in every five years.

Questions

1   Upon what biblical principles would you base the pattern and
style of the preaching in your church?
2   What differences did our Lord and the apostles make in their
approach to different kinds of people?

25.
Training and sending

Elders are responsible to ensure that so far as possible people in the church are trained (Ephesians 4:12) for the work they are expected to do, and that there is a continuing expectation that members will be sent to Christian work in other places.

Training

Work in house groups and auxiliaries will often be a training ground for future elders and deacons, or evangelists to be sent out by the church to other areas; this training should not be accidental but a positive aim of the elders. When members show promise in a certain type of work such as radio or television, bible teaching or work in ethnic groups they should be guided towards the development of their talent. Reading can be suggested, courses can be pursued and in some cases residential college training may be appropriate.

Some training in bible knowledge and theology may be catered for in courses run by a church or by a group of churches. When there are professional people in the church such as teachers, scientists, psychologists, the elders should consider if this is the Lord's provision for them to provide courses for their own church or members from other fellowships.

An area often neglected is the training of house group leaders. They need to know how to conduct conversational bible study and discussion in such a way as to stop talkative people saying too much, and others saying too little, and to draw out response from all present in an atmosphere of liberty and openness.

Elders themselves need to be well equipped for their task. Those who have had formal training in a college or some other course, should still keep themselves refreshed in their reading and by regular attendance at conferences. It has been said the worst thing that can happen to a preaching elder is that he has stopped reading. I would add, that he has also stopped consulting with others. Those without formal training could benefit from day courses at which they meet with colleagues from other churches. This is happening in some areas for both elders and deacons, and could profitably be taken up by others.

Sending out workers

These could be evangelists in their own country or overseas, or people to take up eldership responsibilities in other churches. Elders should take great care when recommending people for Christian work in social and caring situations. Even more care is needed in sending out people into specifically spiritual ministries.

In this context the spiritual condition of the local church is of the utmost importance. The church at Lystra was spiritually strong in that, though it was newly formed, an eldership was established (Acts 14:21-23); this church was able to commend Timothy for work with Paul (Acts 16:1-2) and was identified in sending Timothy out, (1 Timothy 4:14). Both the example of Lystra and of Antioch (Acts 13:1-3) indicate that it is the local church's responsibility to send out evangelists, and this must never be handed over to organisations outside of the local church.

Evangelists normally arise in evangelistic churches. Just as parental responsibilities begin before a baby is born, in the establishing of a healthy atmosphere into which the child will come, so the spiritual atmosphere of a church and its evangelistic zeal are necessary preparations for the sending out of evangelists. Such churches will be instructed in the biblical principles of mission as much as in all other doctrines; it is too late to begin such instruction when a member is being considered for sending out. It takes time to prepare a church to be ready to face this kind of challenge.

The church at Lystra was certainly not without missionary information, and it is well that information about what God is doing in various places is kept before the church. Also the church owes it to its young people to give them the feel and experience of outreach work in many forms. It is in this kind of setting that elders should be prayerfully alert to the Holy Spirit's gifting of the members, and to provide opportunities for them to be exercised and developed.

The sending of a worker can be initiated in a number of ways. It can begin by the Spirit's work in the heart of a member, but the first move could be by the elders having discerned that a member has suitable gifts and then challenging that person to consider the matter. Again, the request of a church or evangelistic organisation for a person to be set apart for certain work could begin the process. The order of these is not important, and they may occur more or less simultaneously; the Holy Spirit has no set patterns of work.

The Holy Spirit may move in the mind and heart of a member by the stirring of his or her conscience about obedience to the Lord's commission. The member may have an urge that is not satisfied in the normal run of church life to make Christ known, perhaps to certain people. The member may realise that he or she has certain qualifications suitable for gospel work and has a strong desire to use them. Sometimes the Lord may bring a member to a 'cross-roads' in life making the person consider the direction and use of life. Most often the Lord uses more than one of these promptings over a period of time.

As with the appointment of elders, a claim to have 'a call' to certain work must be tested in the light of Scripture and the requirements of the task. Where necessary a church must be willing gently but firmly, to advise a person claiming a call that in the view of the church this claim is mistaken.

As the church, led by the elders, considers a person for evangelistic work some specific questions must be answered. Has this person recognisable godliness? Is there zeal for sound doctrine, the building up of churches and the honour of Christ? This applies whether or not the work to be done is actual preaching or some kind of support ministry. Is there love for the lost and for Christ? (2 Corinthians 5:14). Is there an established faith in the Lord and in the power of his Word?

Normally there will have been a useful period of work in church life. No one is likely to be more effective simply for having changed from part-time to full-time service, and from service in their home church to an overseas situation. This period of church life will have shown up if the person is able to work with others, and is reliable.

Remember experience shows that missionaries have rarely been easy to work with — pioneers have to be somewhat headstrong! There must be a clear assessment of the gifts and qualities required in the particular work and place contemplated. It may be that if these abilities are not evident already, they could be developed through training and experience. Failures are not required, but learners are. The question of physical health and emotional stability must be honestly faced but care is needed in evaluating the evidence; the Lord has used many a 'creaking gate'. All this requires time for the church to know the person and to discover all possible information about the nature of the field of work and about training that may be necessary to complete preparation.

After the evangelist has been sent out the church has the responsibility to continue its pastoral care. The person's own church is best placed to take a particular and personal interest in the welfare of its member. This care should involve regular two-way correspondence and reports from the worker; the church should be sensitive to the spiritual needs of its member especially when he or she is in an isolated situation without the opportunity to receive ministry. Tapes of ministry and subscriptions to magazines may well be much appreciated. The pastoral welfare of the worker should be discussed regularly by the elders and the whole church.

Overseas workers are not special people, they are flesh and blood and are just as sensitive to unwise words and actions as any elder or member at home. While we have a right to expect them to be mature believers we must bear in mind that they are subject to depression, discouragement, staleness and all the other problems common to Christian workers, but often they cannot share them with any one else. Happy the missionary who can write to his sending church and say: 'I rejoice greatly in the Lord that you have renewed your concern for me' (Philippians 4:10).

Questions

1   Upon what principles would you decide the kind of training needed for different kinds of work?
2   How can your church help to produce more Christian workers to meet the worldwide needs of Christ's kingdom today?

26.
Prayer and revival

Prayer

It must be obvious that the prayer life of the church is of paramount importance. Elders should make the church aware of this in their teaching, in their example, and in the priorities they set in the overall structure of the church. There is always a need for the church as a whole to meet regularly for prayer, and members who are careless about this should be made aware of their own loss and the fact that they are depriving the church of something essential to its well-being. Legalism must be avoided and undue pressure should not be brought to bear upon people whose hearts are right but whose circumstances prevent their attendance.

The regular church prayer meeting is only part of the prayer life of the church. Elders should encourage private prayer for specific objectives. Older or infirm people who cannot be active in the service of the church should be given a place of importance as praying partners. This should not be vaguely referred to but seen as a positive ministry alongside teachers, musicians and others.

Also members should be encouraged to pray together in each others' homes when they meet informally or by specific arrangements; and there should be gatherings for prayer for certain needs. As the Lord gives the burden so groups can be called together to intercede for people with special problems, for events in the church, for missionary enterprise, and many other things. In my own church there is a regular prayer meeting for the conversion of relatives of church members. The whole church should be bathed in prayer.

Elders need to encourage all members to take part in prayer. This is not to oppress those who are naturally shy and make them feel embarrassed, or even cause them to stay away. Home groups and smaller meetings are often the occasion for those who are less confident and shy of mature members to begin to express themselves in prayer. This is frequently a great blessing to others. Elders and group leaders also need to prevent certain people from lengthy prayers. These have a deadening effect on a prayer meeting and add a further problem to those who want to offer a sentence of prayer but are too embarrassed to do so. I once had a group of young people tell me they could never pray in the prayer meeting because they couldn't pray for ten minutes or more like the men who normally took part. They were amazed when I told them how pleased I was! I asked them to promise that at the next prayer meeting they would each offer one sentence, and say Amen. In the event, all of them managed more than one sentence, but the effect was a lasting transformation of the prayer meeting in that church.

As in everything else we can stifle the Holy Spirit. He can take hold of a meeting in such a way that 'time and sense seem all no more'. Elders need discernment here.

Prayer meetings sometimes become rather feeble. We are given a list of needs of members or of others in whom the church has an interest. We deliver our 'shopping list' and then go home. There is nothing at all wrong in making our wants and wishes known to the Lord and to look for his answers to those prayers; this is not to be despised, rather encouraged. But there are notes missing in such prayer meetings to the loss of the church. One is worship. A pastor friend once said to me, 'Oh! for some God-centred praying in my prayer meeting.' What he meant was more thanksgiving, more worship and praise. There was a time when physical and material needs were rarely mentioned in prayer meetings; now it is possible for there to be little else. The prayers of Paul give us an example of thanksgiving and of prayers for the spiritual life of each of our fellow believers which we rarely follow (Ephesians 1:15-23; 3:14-21; Colossians 1:3-13).

Another missing element in our prayer meetings is conflict. Prayer is a weapon (2 Corinthians 10:4; Ephesians 6:18) and Paul called his prayer life an energetic struggle against the powers of evil (Colossians 1:24-2:1). In our prayer meetings we rarely feel this atmosphere of warfare. Elders need to lead the church in this, laying hold on the power of God and seeking the defeat of Christ's enemies in the world. Paul says that our spiritual weapons 'have divine power to demolish strongholds' (2 Corinthians 10:4).

If the body of the local church is to be healthy it must breathe and prayer is the 'breath of God returning whence it came'.

Revival

Elders cannot be responsible for producing a spiritual awakening. The risen and glorified Christ alone can pour out his Spirit upon a church or community.

However, I do believe it is the duty of elders to encourage the church to pray for greater spiritual power to be felt in the church and to expect the Lord to answer that prayer in some measure at some time. We ought not to allow a church to settle down to quiet orthodoxy and uneventful normality. Elders should seek the removal of traditionalism, division, and anything else that 'puts out the Spirit's fire' (1 Thessalonians 5:19). They should strive by prayer and exhortation to encourage an atmosphere of spiritual sensitivity and expectancy. No matter how much blessing we receive in terms of conversions and the building up of the membership, our church life will be like a desert in comparison with the streams of spiritual life that flow in times of revival. A church is a spiritual body. When the Lord made man he formed him 'from the dust of the ground'. In one sense man was a well organised structure. But then 'God breathed into his nostrils the breath of life and the man became a living being' (Genesis 2:7). We may belong to the best of churches, but we still need to pray as we sing, 'O Breath of Life come sweeping through us'.

No matter whether or not we feel free to apply Revelation 3:20 as an appeal to unbelievers, no one will disagree that the primary message of this text was to a church. There is no church that is so blessed that it has no need to respond to the Lord's words, 'Those whom I love I rebuke and discipline. So be earnest and repent. Here I am, I stand at the door and knock. If anyone hears my voice and opens the door, I will come in and eat with him and he with me.' (See also John 14:23; Malachi 3:10.)

There is a realised presence of our Lord, a bright shining of his face, a demonstration of his love and power, beyond the normal experience of our church life. This is not to be worked up but prayed for and looked for. If the church is aware that the elders are serious about such expectation, then the members too will join in the cry to the Lord to 'rend the heavens and come down' (Isaiah 64:1).

Questions

1   What can be done to make your prayer meetings a powerful weapon in the spiritual conflict today?
2   How can prayer for revival be stimulated without distracting attention from immediate responsibilities?

27.
Relationship of members to elders

As citizens we are commanded to pray for those in authority (1 Timothy 2:1-2). Nevertheless it seems part of human nature to complain about 'them' because 'they' are always making silly decisions, and surely a change of government couldn't make things worse!

Such attitudes should be completely foreign to church life. There are two extremes to be avoided; on the one hand members should not put their leaders on pedestals as though they were little gods. This is wrong in principle because idolatry is forbidden in Scripture. It is bad for the leaders because it tempts them to pride and a feeling of infallibility. They will also resent being questioned. Such idolising is bad for the church because decisions made will lack the backing of adequate questioning and research. It also results in a great shock all round when the shortcomings and failings of the leaders are eventually exposed; they fall from the pedestal — and great is their fall.

In the other extreme, members treat their leaders with contempt. The leaders can do nothing right and the members constantly criticise, undermine what the leaders are trying to do, and create an unhelpful, unfruitful atmosphere in the church. These extremes are quite foreign to the Scriptures which set before us a different attitude altogether.

All leaders are human and a healthy approach is to recognise their weaknesses and to try to cover those weaknesses with prayer and loving support and encouragement.

The members are exhorted to 'respect those who work hard

among you, who are over you in the Lord and admonish you' (1
Thessalonians 5:12). The meaning of this respect is to recognise
their worth and the value of their work. Elders must earn this esteem
by their diligence and faithfulness (Philippians 2:29-30). In 1
Thessalonians 5:13 Paul goes on to say: 'Hold them in the highest
regard in love because of their work. Live in peace with each other'.
The relationship between members and leaders can be likened to a
marriage; the submission of members like the submission of wives
is one of loving respect. It is not unquestioning, servile submission
but intelligent, affectionate acceptance of leadership. Such love and
esteem is not blind to faults, but helps the other to overcome them.
It does not magnify their shortcomings or harp on them but covers
them. Also Christians are best able to receive teaching and especially correction from people they love and respect, and whom they
know love and respect them (Proverbs 27:6).

If members recognise the validity of the work elders do they will
not behave as though the elders do not exist. Members will seek the
help and counsel of their leaders and value the advice given. It is a
pity if there is an over reaction against the 'heavy shepherding'
which occurs in some circles. Elders have no authority to direct
members in the personal conduct and decisions in their lives; but in
an atmosphere of loving confidence members should be encouraged
to share decision making and other concerns with their leaders.

When members respect their leaders they do not criticise them
among neighbours and in their families. We cannot expect our
friends or our children to be drawn to the church if we show little
regard for those who lead it and constantly question their motives
and actions.

In 1 Timothy 5:17-18 Paul says, 'The elders who direct the
affairs of the church well are worthy of double honour, especially
those whose work is preaching and teaching. For the Scripture says,
"Do not muzzle the ox while it is treading out the grain", and "The
workman deserves his wages".' There is no doubt that the 'double
honour' is provision for the material needs of those who give their
whole time to the service of the church. When a church sets apart a
'full-time' worker the financial and material commitment should be
honouring to the Lord. It should not be as little as possible but as
much as possible. A full-time worker's standard of living should not
be markedly lower or markedly higher than the average of the
congregation. I hope the days are far gone when members said,

'keep him poor and he will work harder'. This was not only immoral it was ineffective. If you starve the ox it will not work! But if you relieve full-time men from more than normal concern about 'making ends meet' you will then release them for prayer, the study of the Word, pastoral ministry and the relaxation to which all are entitled.

Through the prophet Malachi (3:10) God said the people were robbing him by failing to give their tithes and offerings. A large proportion of those tithes and offerings were to maintain the Old Testament priesthood (1 Corinthians 9:11-14). Failure to do this was robbing God, but it was also robbing themselves. There is a distinct connection between the faithfulness of the people in their support of the priests and the Lord opening 'the floodgates of heaven' in revival blessings (Galatians 6:6-10).

Obedience and submission of members to their leaders is clearly taught in Hebrews 13:17. Again we see the need for elders to merit the loyalty of their flock as they watch over them 'as men who must give an accoount.' The words obedience and submission are used in connection with marriage (1 Peter 3:5-6). Members are to follow the lead given by elders in an attitude of love and respect and in the liberty of prayerful discussion and mutual submission to Christ as Lord. Unquestioning obedience is not required and it can never bring people to maturity in Christ (Ephesians 4:13) because they are putting their faith in the church rather than in the Lord.

Members should encourage their leaders by a timely, cheerful word, a smile and not a scowl, and by commitment to the Lord, his people and the work. Sometimes members assume their elders are above the normal stresses of discouragement and disappointment. We should remember our leaders are like Elijah, 'a man just like us' (James 5:17) and that most probably they are bearing a greater than normal burden because of their spiritual responsibilities. An elder may become depressed because of lack of relaxation, loneliness, pressure in the home, the demands of preaching, the attacks of Satan and even the 'super successful' ministry of others. Elders need encouragement.

An anonymous writer in *Grace* Magazine offered some very practical hints as to how members can encourage elders.

'The people listened attentively' (Nehemiah 8:3). It is very difficult to listen to the preaching of God's word attentively if you come to God's house ill-prepared and in the wrong frame of mind. If you have not prepared at home before you come, ten seconds with head bowed when you arrive will not do it for you. It is important to be early so as to prepare for worship and the preaching of God's word. There is nothing that so encourages a preacher as to know he has a congregation eager to hear God's word. Come to church with expectancy and praying that God would visit the congregation with his blessing.

Do not discuss 'big issues' with the preacher just before the service. He can easily be 'put off' as he seeks to lead the congregation to God's throne, and that will affect the whole of the congregation. After the service, if God has blessed you in it, say 'Thank you' to the preacher but don't overdo it so it becomes flattery. If God has blessed you through the preaching share that blessing with the preacher. What he may have considered to be his worst pulpit utterance may have been of enormous help to you. Tell him, it will humble him, for he is in God's hands, and it will encourage him.

But the greatest way to encourage a preacher is for him to see you putting God's word into practice in your daily life as you see its importance for you and for others. Bringing those others to hear God's word will also be a great encouragement to the man of God. Never go to a gospel service alone. You have great opportunities to bring your daily contacts under the preaching of God's word each week.

Many pastors today are overburdened with lengthy bouts of pastoral counselling which consume their time and drain their energy. Much of the reason for this is that the word preached has not been attended to (it has not been listened to attentively) and has not been applied to daily life in obedience. Disobedience brings an inevitable crop of problems in its train. When going to your pastor with a problem, examine your own life first to see if a basic biblical principle is being violated which is causing the problem. Although pastors can be wrong (they're only human), not to take their advice and to end up in a further mess can cause all manner of frustrations for the shepherd of God's flock. He is not a pastor without his gifts of shepherding having been first tested in some way or another. Failing to heed his advice is undermining his ministry, and questioning his role in the church.

A pastor is a human being. His workload is as heavy as, and often heavier than, most other men in society. He does not have the usual five-day week of the rest of society, so you should respect the one day off he has in the week. At least one church known to the writer diverts all the telephone calls on that day. Remember above all that he is a human being and needs time with his family just as you do (otherwise he will have problem children).

He needs to spend time with his wife (otherwise she will be a pastor's widow). He needs time to preach elsewhere (otherwise he will become narrow and insular). He needs time for holidays and conferences (otherwise you will suffer from a stale ministry). He needs time for his own interests, hobbies, and recreational pursuits (otherwise he becomes unbalanced). All these things are essential, otherwise your pastor will face exhaustion, as many have, and do, although that was never intended by their church members.

Most of all and above all, a praying people is a tremendous encouragement to a pastor. C. H. Spurgeon, who had such gifts and such a great intellect, when asked for the secret of his success replied, 'My people pray for me.' That mattered most to him, and matters most to men of today. If the Apostle Paul needed the prayers of the people (Ephesians 6:19) for him as a person, so do the pastors of today — 'Pray also for me.' A church which prays for its pastor will be blessed as God answers its prayers. It will love its pastor and support him, because it speaks to God regularly about him. He'll be a better man for your prayers, and will stay with you to serve his master with greater joy and zeal.

We should also constantly pray that our elders will be protected from Satan's attacks and from sin itself, and that they will remain faithful to God and his Word.

We should ask the Lord to keep our elders from becoming more concerned about their position than with serving the Lord. They need us to pray that the Lord will give them wisdom and diligence in guarding and helping the flock, and also the ability to encourage and comfort those in trouble. They need our prayers that they will

be able to minister the Word of God powerfully and effectively
(1 Thessalonians 1:5; Ephesians 6:19-20).

John Benton writes, 'Happy is the church where the people love
the elders and the elders love the people, and they all love the Lord!
Watch such a church — good things are bound to happen.'

Questions

1   If an elder refuses to listen to reasonable criticism what can be
done about it?
2   What principles should govern the giving of a sabbatical (a
period of months free from pastoral responsibilies) to an elder?

28.
Relationship of members to members

A good relationship between the members of the church will arise from the example set by the elders, but they must also expound to the church those scriptures that set out how members should relate to each other. Hebrews 10:24-25 brings together many of the elements in this relationship.

Think it through

'Let us consider how...' As with a marriage, good relationships within a church don't happen automatically. They have to be thought through and worked at. Paul wrote to the Philippians 'Each of you should look not only to your own interests but also to the interests of others' (Philippians 2:4). There are two emphases in Hebrews 10:24. One is persistence. We are to pay constant attention to the needs of our fellow members. We must not give them mere occasional thought or passing interest; concern for each other's material and spiritual welfare is to be the very fibre of church life. The other emphasis is depth of concern. The word 'consider' implies concentration. We are not allowed to escape with a passing 'How are you?' — with no real concern or intention of doing anything about the answer we receive. Often people do not bother to tell the truth about their circumstances or their spiritual well-being because they know help will not be forthcoming. Our friends need to know that we are genuinely concerned for them and will give a practical response to what they say. Others are naturally reticent

158 Only servants

to speak of themselves but the Lord doesn't excuse us from our obligations to them. We must get alongside people, not to probe into their private affairs or become busybodies, but to give them confidence to share their needs with us. It may also be that if we 'consider' our friends constantly and deeply we will see needs they are not aware of. This places us under an obligation to help them see that need and answer it.

Spur one another on

Too often we dampen the zeal of other members. Hebrews 10:24 tells us we must 'spur one another on to love and good deeds'. This includes stimulating each other in our witness to non-christians, to love them and show that love in practical kindness and good neighbourliness. But it also applies to activity between members. By example and by exhortation we are to develop a loving and a caring fellowship. The example of our Lord in John 13:1-17 challenges us. Jesus was a servant to his disciples by washing their feet of the filth from the journey on the Palestinian roads. Then he said, 'I have set you an example that you should do as I have done for you.' This sets for us the pattern of making sure that every member in the church is cared for. We are to relieve the burdens of mothers with young children, of those who are ill and the elderly. Where members are overwhelmed with problems we are to be at their side — 'let us not love with words or tongue but with actions and in truth' (1 John 3:18).

An essential element in our loving relationship is asking for forgiveness and forgiving each other. Generally speaking we are not very good at this. Perhaps that is why the Scripture refers to the matter so often. 'Be kind and compassionate to one another, forgiving each other, just as in Christ God forgave you. Be imitators of God, therefore, as dearly loved children' (Ephesians 4:32-5:1). Jesus Christ is devastating on this subject: 'If you forgive men when they sin against you your heavenly Father will also forgive you. But if you do not forgive men their sins your Father will not forgive your sins' (Matthew 6:14-15). This is not salvation by works, but it is a requirement that our profession of faith shows its reality in Christlikeness. If we will not forgive others we have to ask ourselves if we are Christians at all.

I believe this is so important we should pursue it a little further. When a relationship is broken we must seek to be reconciled. This means an apology must be offered and an assurance of forgiveness given. It requires two to make a quarrel and two to repair the damage. Our offer of an apology may be met with a rebuff, in that case we must ask the Lord to intervene for us and enable us to work for the restoration of harmony. If we have been offended I believe we should forgive even in the absence of an apology. I respect the views of those who disagree with this, but I am persuaded that a forgiving spirit shown to those who offend us is more likely to produce an apology at last, than many appeals for repentance. True we may need at times to remonstrate with a brother or sister to help them see their mistake or their fault. But our forgiveness should not depend on their repentance. God's forgiveness of us follows our repentance but he is our Judge — we are not judges, we are brothers and sisters in Christ.

Another scripture that challenges us is Matthew 5:23-24: 'If you are offering your gift at the altar and there remember that your brother has something against you, leave the gift there in front of the altar; first go and be reconciled to your brother, then come and offer your gift.' Notice this is not a case of being offended — but realising we have given offence to someone else. A brother or sister is nursing a grievance against us. We do not have the option of saying, 'my conscience is clear', nor of waiting for them to approach us. It may be that we have obstinately refused to admit that the fault could be ours. Whatever the reason, there is a break of fellowship and we have to do something about it. The Lord's words in Matthew 5:23-24 suggest that God will not listen to our prayers or receive our worship until we have done our part toward reconciliation.

Encourage one another

The inter-action of member with member also includes encouraging one another (Hebrews 10:25). We can link this with a number of other passages of Scripture, Romans 15:14; Ephesians 4:16; 5:18-21; Colossians 3:16; 1 Thessalonians 4:18; Hebrews 3:13. If we put together the strands of thought in these verses we see that our responsibilities to other members include encouragement, comfort, edifying, warning, exhortation and correction. And all this is to be conducted in an atmosphere of love and thanksgiving to God. This ministry is not to be left to the elders. It is the responsibility of members to each other, helped and encouraged in it by the elders. Every Sunday morning I see a teenage daughter carry her little brother from the service to the creche. The wise mother does not do everything herself but encourages the members of the family to help each other. The example is a good one for elders to follow (or maybe some parents could learn this from the example of wise elders!).

We sometimes use the word 'fellowship' in a very limited way. We have a meal together or watch a missionary video in company with other Christians. For many Christians this is the limit of their understanding of fellowship. A responsibility of elders is to show members how to minister to one another in both material and spiritual things. Organised fellowship groups within the church are useful opportunities to exercise this mutual ministry. But such fellowship should become a spontaneous outflow of love among members all the time. The answer to Cain's question, 'Am I my brother's keeper?' is a resounding 'Yes'.

Probably the most difficult area, and therefore the most neglected, is that of warning or correction. We are afraid of this because of the temptation to censoriousness and pride, and also the possibility that our stumbling efforts may be rebuffed. We leave such things to the elders with the result that the situation has become very much more difficult to handle by the time the elders are even aware of the problem.

Two parabolic illustrations in the New Testament throw light on this matter. They are found in John 13:1-17 and Matthew 7:3-5. We have already referred to John 13:1-17 and to our Lord's example there of humble practical service to his disciples. We need no other incentive to care for the material needs of our fellow members, but we must not limit the application of this passage to bearing each other's physical and material burdens. Jesus himself used the washing of the disciples feet to illustrate our need of spiritual cleansing — 'A person who has had a bath needs only to wash his feet' (v.10); this meant that if we are regenerate — washed in the bath — we need only to be cleansed from the defilements we pick up on life's road — our feet washed. The Lord went on to say 'I have set you an example' and that must mean we have a responsibility to seek the cleansing of our brothers and sisters in Christ. This has to be done through teaching, warning and correcting. Two hazards immediately come to view. One is that our brother or sister may refuse this 'foot washing' as Peter did at first. When this happens we must resort to prayer and maybe consult other mature members or our elders. The other hazard is the possibility of our own unwillingness to receive rebuke or warning from others. We may say, I can take it from the pastor, but not from anyone else. Some of us are willing to be frank with others but resent them being frank with us. Every aspect of the Christian life has hazards and the higher up the spiritual mountain we climb the stronger the wind blows. But we cannot escape the Lord's requirement — 'I have set you an example'.

The parabolic illustration in Matthew 7:3-5 places us under the same obligation.

> Why do you look at the speck of sawdust in your brother's eye and pay no attention to the plank in your own eye? How can you say to your brother, 'Let me take the speck out of your eye,' when all the time there is a plank in your own eye? You hypocrite, first take the plank out of your own eye, and then you will see clearly to remove the speck from your brother's eye.

Warning and correction are illustrated in taking a speck out of someone else's eye. The Lord's main lesson is that we first must rid ourselves of the plank of pride or censoriousness before we can exercise a correction ministry to others. That is where most of us stop; but the Lord did not stop there. We are to deal with ourselves and then we are to seek grace to help our fellow members when occasion requires; we then see the task is as delicate as trying to take a speck out of someone's eye. For example, we need to have a sure touch. This means we must know how the scriptures apply to the specific problem. This is our only authority. We must approach the task with prayer, relying on the Holy Spirit. True love will make us humble and gentle but firm and positive.

Meet often

We will only be able to minister to each other if we meet frequently. 'Let us not give up meeting together' (Hebrews 10:25). This applies not only to regular formal meetings but also to informal encounters.

We need to meet with others for them to minister to us as well as giving us opportunities to minister to them. The obligation to meet together is a requirement of the Lord, but our obedience should be motivated by love to him and love to our brothers and sisters in the church. If we absent ourselves we deprive others of the blessing we should be to them, and we rob ourselves of the good others can do to us.

All this is involved in the ministry of 'pastors and teachers' as defined by Paul in Ephesians 4:12, 'to prepare God's people for works of service, so that the body of Christ may be built up'.

Questions

1 How can informal spiritual fellowship be stimulated among the members of your church?
2 How can your church members be made more caring towards each other?

29.
Crisis point

There is sometimes a moment in the life of a Christian leader when all seems to be lost and the only solution is to give up. This may be compounded by the physical results of stress or strain, and resignation appears to be the only resort. Some men of God in Scripture had this kind of experience. For instance, Jeremiah lamented he had agreed to be a prophet (Jeremiah 20:7-18), and Jonah could not cope with his situation for very different reasons (Jonah 4:1-3). Such situations may result in a resignation, or they may be resolved by the man standing firm and bearing the consequences. Paul worked out the tensions between himself and the Corinthian church in 2 Corinthians 10-12. Our Lord himself agonised in Gethsemane, before the Cross (Luke 22:42-44), and many a time a leader has borrowed the Lord's words 'Not my will but yours be done' in situations of great distress.

By 'crisis point' I mean a complete breakdown of relationship between a church and its leader or leaders. The reasons for such breakdowns are many but perhaps I can underline three major causes.

The first is immorality on the part of a leader. The second is the effect of rapid changes in evangelical church life, worship, evangelism, administration, preaching and teaching. Sometimes an elder wants changes the church is not willing to make. At other times the church becomes impatient with a leadership that is reluctant to agree to changes. A third reason for crises arising is the apparent inability of leaders to understand their people. Sometimes they are deaf to what the church is saying, or fail to take seriously rumblings of discontent. They trade on the love and goodwill of the people, or they wrongly interpret questionings as evidence of lack of these graces. They do not understand that members are saying 'We love our pastor — our elders — we don't want to be disloyal, but... but...' Often it is sheer stupidity that we are surprised when a crisis develops.

Preventing it

Leaders need to recognise the dangers lurking for them in the lowered morality of our times. They should walk close to the Lord, pray for each other and be watchful for themselves and their colleagues, and be careful about pastoral counselling situations, especially where emotions may run high. Our calling is an emotional one and we are to be sympathetic and tender to those to whom we minister; therein lies the peril for the unwary.

Many other crisis situations can be prevented if adequate care is taken before an elder is appointed. This is especially applicable when a man is invited from outside the membership. As we have seen, he needs to know a lot about the church, its history, its ethos, its weaknesses and strengths, and its hopes and aspirations. Also the church should find out about the man, his doctrines, his character, his leadership qualities, his preaching, his special interests, and his wife and family.

Then there are spiritual preventatives. Physically we keep our bodies healthy to reduce the possibility of serious breakdown. Likewise a church needs to keep its spiritual life healthy. Concentration on evangelism and worship, but failure to strengthen the spiritual life of the church within its relationships will all too easily leave the church open to crisis. An essential part of the teaching ministry is to deal with great New Testament passages that show what a church should be like (Romans 15:14; 1 Corinthians chapters 11 — 14; Ephesians 4:1-16; Philippians 2: 1-16; Hebrews 10:24-25; 1 John 3:11-18). But teaching is not enough, prayerful mutual ministry and fellowship, and love among the members has to be encouraged. Also the church should become accustomed to submitting everything to the authority of Scripture so that teaching and decision making are freed from personal opinions and preferences so far as possible.

But no matter how healthy a church becomes crises may still occur. Indeed the Evil One will see to it that something with potential danger intrudes. We should not be surprised or be taken unawares. It happened in the early church and will happen until the day of grace ends.

Leaders need to be sensitive to signs of a potential crisis and to take positive steps to avert it. Perhaps in some situations a crisis resulting in division and defections must happen because of departure from sound doctrine or ungodly conduct. But often it is possible to see signs of dissension about less fundamental issues. Members become restive in a church meeting; a critical spirit begins to creep in; congregations fall in number or the atmosphere becomes cold; prayer meetings lack vitality, or a general unwillingness to be committed to the work. These and many other signs should be noticed by elders in the early stages. The great danger is to ignore them and hope they will go away. As with a cancer, the earlier treatment begins the greater the possibility of a cure.

When warning signs occur the members should be made aware that the elders have seen them. Let there be a call to prayer and humiliation before God, then let there be open and frank discussion.

'If we walk in the light, as he is in the light, we have fellowship with one another, and the blood of Jesus, his Son, purifies us from all sin' (1 John 1:7).

Handling it

If an elder falls into immorality, he is subject to the disciplines we have already discussed in chapter twenty-one. He should not wait to be asked to relinquish his ministry but rather tender his resignation voluntarily. This saves the church some of the inevitable pain. Fellow elders or colleagues from other churches must wrap such a person round with love and understanding, and seek to recover the situation and restore the one who has sinned. In my view this does not include restoration to eldership, but that view is not shared by all.

Where a crisis has other causes, and there is but one elder in the church, it will almost certainly be necessary to seek the help of a brother minister or a recognised 'association' representative. A danger that must be avoided is for only one side of the problem to be heard. If possible whoever is asked to intervene should have the confidence of the leaders and the church, and care must be taken to listen to all sides of the contention. Where there is a plural eldership or a strong diaconate it should be possible for the matter to be handled within the church unless the disagreement is between the leaders themselves. We have discussed this problem in chapter seventeen.

It is impossible to lay down a procedure to be followed in such crises. Circumstances and personalities differ so much that the wisdom of experience and above all the guidance of the Holy Spirit are the essential needs. But the following guidelines may be helpful:

1. For the honour of Christ and the health of the churches every effort must be made to heal the breach. Therefore hasty decisions should be avoided at all costs, and if possible there should be a 'cooling off' period.

2. A church needs to remember that they appointed the leader or leaders in question and so share the responsibility if a mistake was made.

3. A man cannot blame the church if he has tried to force on it radical changes which played no part in the discussion before he was appointed.

4. All concerned need to be reminded that the Christian graces of humility, love, peaceableness and a forgiving spirit, must be exercised to the utmost limit. All discussions should be conducted 'at the foot of the Cross' (Ephesians 4:29-5:2).

5. A very clear distinction must be made between biblical requirements and personal preferences. The need for ultimate parting can only be justified on perceived departure from the Scripture, either by the church or the leadership.

6. A spirit of confession must prevail with all concerned being willing to admit faults and to put them right.

7. All concerned should reflect that the church is not theirs, but the Lord's. His authority must prevail in the doctrines upheld and in the resolving of the matters in dispute.

8. Those who maintain a biblical position should not be the ones to resign. Too often the field is left to those less worthy because those faithful to the Word are not willing to stand firm.

9. An elder who feels he has to maintain his position must examine himself, if necessary with help from honest friends. He must make sure he is not being obstinately blind to his faults that are stumbling the church. He must also be sure, if he is determined to stand firm, that this is for the Lord's honour and not his own reputation. An examination of the history of many a church now thriving will show that the turning point came when a man was prepared to weather the storm, and steer the church to calmer seas.

Healing it

No matter whether a breach has been averted or if all attempts at reconciliation have failed, a healing ministry will be necessary. If the potential division has after all not happened, let there be a spirit of praise and thanksgiving to the Lord. But at the same time many people may have been hurt. They may have sacrificed fondly held views for the sake of harmony. There is the danger of continuing bitterness between those who have been in hot contention. These things must not be neglected in the relief felt at the resolving of the problem. It may be right for a period of time for there to be concentration on a ministry of reconciliation, with all eyes focussed on the Lord and his love for the whole church. No one must be allowed to say, 'I can forgive but I cannot forget', without correction. Such people must be reminded of the Lord's forgiving grace, 'I will forgive their wickedness and will remember their sins no more' (Hebrews 8:12).

When it has not been possible to avoid a breach what I have already said applies to those who remain. In addition, if at all possible, great care must be taken to maintain a loving relationship with those who leave. Every effort should be made to restore them, but where the differences may be irreconcilable, the people themselves should be reconciled.

A church has a special duty towards an elder who resigns or is dismissed. There will be pain, and there may be bitterness. A church should not be careless or hardhearted but broken-hearted in such circumstances, and in a spirit of self-abasement seek to minister to the brother. The greatest pain may be felt by his wife and family and the church must not accept a rebuff from them but try to overcome it with persistent love. If the elder has been full-time and perhaps occupying a house provided by the church, more than adequate material provision should be made over a very reasonable period of time.

All crisis situations should be occasions of humiliation and repentance before the Lord on the part of the whole church. Sometimes, when there has been a marriage breakdown followed by reconciliation the relationship becomes stronger and deeper than it was before. Pray that when churches recover from crises their love and fellowship will be at a level that excels all they had known before.

Questions

1   How can a church be sensitive to the onset of a crisis without looking for trouble?
2   Does your 'devotion' (Romans 12:10) to your brothers and sisters in the church easily wilt under pressure?

Epilogue

Philippians 2:1-16

When Paul was on his way to Rome his ship was wrecked by a severe storm. Some of the sailors tried to escape in a lifeboat, but Paul said, 'Unless these men stay with the ship you cannot be saved' (Acts 27:31).

A local church can be likened to a storm-tossed ship and the concern of the elders and members is that the church will not founder but 'be saved'. This was Paul's meaning when he wrote to the Philippian church, 'My dear friends, as you have always obeyed, not only in my presence but now much more in my absence, continue to work out your salvation with fear and trembling, for it is God who works in you (or, among you) to will and to act according to his good purpose' (vv.12-13).

The apostle was in prison and from a distance could only imagine what was happening. The Philippian church no longer had his presence to guide them and to protect them from mistakes that could cause them to founder. He says, 'be like-minded, having the same love, being one in spirit. Do nothing out of selfish ambition or vain conceit but in humility consider others better than yourselves. Each of you should not only look to your own interests but also to the interests of others' (vv.2-4). Without this kind of thinking, division and discord would ruin the church so Paul gives them the example of Jesus Christ and his humility as their pattern (vv.5-11).

Paul is well aware of the hazards and therefore he exhorts the church to be afraid of making shipwreck and thus giving him pain.

They should tremble at the knowledge of their own weaknesses and the possibility of Satan taking advantage of them. They are to 'work out their salvation with fear and trembling' as children of God. This will be in stark contrast to the atmosphere of the world around them (vv.14-16). When churches led by their elders take seriously the requirements of Scripture, they too will be fearful of offending the Lord and ruining their witness. With the 'mind of Christ' (v.5) they will be as lights in a dark world as they 'hold out the word of life' (v.16).

But 'who is equal to such a task?' (2 Corinthians 2:16). The answer is 'It is God who works in you to will and to act according to his good purpose' (v.13).

Lest anyone should be discouraged by the demands of this 'noble task' I gladly testify that though pressures, burdens and tears abound, fulfilment and reward much more abound.

> I have fought the good fight, I have finished the race, I have kept the faith. Now there is in store for me the crown of righteousness, which the Lord, the righteous judge, will award to me on that day — and not only to me, but also to all who have longed for his appearing (2 Timothy 4:7-8).

> When the Chief Shepherd appears, you will receive the crown of glory that will never fade away (1 Peter 5:4).

> Well done, good and faithful servant! You have been faithful with a few things; I will put you in charge of many things. Come and share your Master's happiness! (Matthew 25:23).

Questions

1 How do you measure success or failure in your work?
2 How do you encourage yourself in the Lord?

Bibliography

Shepherding God's flock	Editor Roger O Beardmore	Sprinkle Publications
A Noble Task	Neil Summerton	Paternoster Press
Skilful Shepherds	Derek Tidball	IVP
God's Plan for the local church	Nigel Lacey	Grace Publications Trust
A guide to pastoral care	R E O White	Pickering and Inglis
Healing the wounded	John White and Ken Blue	IVP
A mind at ease	M L Ashton	Overcomer Literature Trust
Pastors under pressure	Paul Beasley-Murray	Kingsway
Dynamic leadership	Paul Beasley-Murray	Marc

The Baptist	Jack Hoad	Grace Publications Trust
We Believe	A Grace Baptist Confession and Guide to church fellowship	Grace Publications Trust
Building with bananas	Derek & Nancy Copley	Paternoster Press
The works of John Owen Vol.16, pages 2-183		Banner of Truth

Every member serving	Keith Davies	Pamphlets available from Grace Baptist Assembly
Practical problems of establishing an eldership	Clifford Pond	

Towards a fresh look at the diaconate *Women in the church* *Leadership in the church* *Pastoral settlements*	Study pamphlets available from Association of Grace Baptist Churches (South East)

Recent titles

published in the

Great Christian Classics **series**

Not Guilty

An abridged version of the classic *Justification* by James Buchanan, first published in 1867, rewritten for today's readers, with a foreword by Herbert M. Carson.

Where do churches today stand with regard to the doctrine of justification by faith alone? How strong or weak a church is depends a great deal on the centrality of this doctrine in its understanding of Christianity.

It was the realization of the rich fulness of justification which gave Paul such a joyful confidence and impelled him into a passionate devotion to Christ, and also an urgency to make this good news known. It is the same message which will stir forgiven sinners to grateful obedience, and will still set churches on a constructive path of biblical worship and witness.

Paperback   **ISBN 0 94646 222 4**   **96 pages**

Thinking spiritually

'To be carnally minded is death, but to be spiritually minded is life and peace.'

Life... peace... death...! Who would not choose life and peace? So what is spiritual-mindedness? What is meant by life and peace? How are we to know whether we are spiritually-minded or not?

John Owen (1616-1683) is one of the most prominent theologians England has ever had. The *Grace and Duty of being Spiritually Minded* was published in 1681, after illness had caused Owen to spend time meditating upon the importance of spirituality.

Here is an abridgement of Owen's volume, in easier English.

Paperback   **ISBN 0 94646 221 6**   **96 pages**

The experience that counts!

Jonathan Edwards (1703-1758), America's greatest theo-
logian, wrote his *Treatise Concerning Religious Affections*
against the background of the First Great Awakening, the
American equivalent of what the British call the Evangelical
Revival. He preached a series of sermons in 1742/3 dealing
with the subject of distinguishing between true and false
religious experience. The *Treatise* was the text of these sermons revised for publication in 1746, abrigded and presented
here in contemporary English.

What a lot of trouble the Church would have escaped,
if Christians had kept to what Scripture teaches about a true
experience of salvation!

Paperback   **ISBN 0 94646 223 2**   **128 pages**